Self Empowerment -Reset Entrepreneur Secrets

Rev. Dr. Marianne Padjan

Amanda M. Renaud, Bill Walters

Dr. Kimberly Linert, Kylee Leota

Jose Escobar, Stephanie Brandolini

Kaaren Hewitt, Tammy Williams,

Rosemary Ghiz, Tuesday Goodson

Josef Stetter, Maxine Willocks

Michelle Lee Angiolillio

Legal Disclaimer

ENTREPRENEUR SECRETS

~ TABLE OF CONTENTS ~

~TABLE OF CONTENTS ~

~TABLE OF CONTENTS ~

~TABLE OF CONTENTS ~

~DEDICATIONS~

This book is dedicated to all entrepreneurs part-time and full-time. May the force be with you!

Rev. Dr. Marianne

~ACKNOWLEDGEMENTS~

I would like to acknowledge every single entrepreneur who has tried to make their dream of being an entrepreneur, true. Congratulations to the ones that actually are entrepreneurs and stuck with it. Being an entrepreneur at times can be nothing more than a glorified job. Other times, it can be amazing and often allows people to live out there wildest dreams. You may also find your biggest purpose.

Thank you to all entrepreneurs!!

Love, light and peace
REV. DR. MARIANNE

~FOREWORD~

Michelle Lee Angiolillo

Are you an entrepreneur just starting out? Or maybe you have been an entrepreneur for many years and now you are ready to take your business to the next level? Whatever your journey is, you have landed in the right place! Lets face it, building your own business can be hard and sometimes lonely. You have in your hands access to a community of people who have been there and are ready to share their secrets with you. Entrepreneur Secrets is a book of entrepreneurs that are dedicated to helping others succeed by sharing their stories in hopes that you can avoid some of the pain they have endured on their journeys while building their dreams.

The stories in this book will touch your heart, inspire you, and empower you to keep fighting for your dreams! Whenever it gets hard and you are ready to give up, remember your WHY. Remember the secrets and stories from this book, keep it close and read it often. The authors in this book believe in you. The authors also hope that their stories will give you the hope, inspiration, and courage needed to keep pushing forward and make your dreams a reality!!!

Michelle Lee Angiolillo

3x International Best-selling Author, Speaker, and Certified Trainer
https://codebreakerglobal.com/crackyourcode?code=michellelee

~ INTRODUCTION~

Rev. Dr. Marianne Padjan

The amazing authors of this book have come together to help educate, inspire—both future and current entrepreneurs. The life of an entrepreneur isn't the easiest path to take and requires a tremendous amount of faith, courage, and confidence. It is extremely rewarding either, because either you learn or you succeed. Either way you will always walk away much wealthier in knowledge and experience. Entrepreneurship has a way of showing you whether or not you are in the right space. At times you are simply purchasing and creating yourself a job.

When things work out for the best, you are always a successful leader for yourself and others. The rocky road of Entrepreneurship certainly has its challenges and is not for an overly sensitive heart. For those wondering what it's like and have never tried it, you will certainly get a great idea after reading this book of what it must be like. Sometimes we have to do a variety of different things, that have nothing to do with business. We do this to make steps forward, such as forgiveness. Unforgiveness is a heavyweight to be carrying around. It is capable of blocking all kinds of interactions and exchanges. Learning to let go of various emotions, thoughts and most frequently people. All of these are a big part of what we do in life. Entrepreneurship is no different. Thank you for reading this book!

~ CHAPTER 1 ~

My Secret is YOU!

Rev. Dr Marianne Padjan

I love the name entrepreneur secrets! I suppose that my secrets are all the things that actually, went right. What about all the things that went wrong? I would say that those have been an even bigger lesson. The ability to avoid making that many mistakes and having to learn from them would have saved so much more time, energy, and money. I truly do believe that we need both.

This whole concept brings me to one of my favorite secrets for entrepreneurs. The number one secret is you absolutely need to get a coach. Yes you will pay the coach but you will save so much energy and money that is how you avoid all of the things that could potentially go wrong or at least mostly. That's for sure will save you a lot of headaches and your business will take off quicker stronger and better! This is the reason we go to summits conferences, seminars, and masterminds its why we join group coaching and one-on-one coaching as well. Learning from others is just an easier path—isn't it?

I guess you could go the harder way and choose the longer less gracious path to success if you want to do that. If you're like most you will prefer the shorter less rocky path to success.

ENTREPRENEUR SECRETS

If your ego needs to think and feel like it did this all on its own, without any help then go forth and do what you need to do I suppose. I m not saying that if you get coached by others. This doesn't mean you will never make a mistake ever again. You will always have a couple of Pebbles on the road to success that you need to deal with. I am just saying make it easier where you can. I believe franchises were born out of this very idea.

Get help and get trained. You don't need to be trained in every little thing, because that brings me to my next secret— that is not a secret. I believe that by now most of us have heard that in order to be successful you really should work from the heart and you should do what your heart feels drawn to. So why would you spend all this time doing all these crazy things you don't like doing. If you need technology but you're not a tech Guru, hire the job out.

If you're not a social media Guru and you need social media to grow your business, hire the job out. If somewhere along the line you need an editor and you don't like reading or writing content out. HIRE OUT! Maybe you need a cleaning lady, because you don't like cleaning- HIRE the job out!!!! I can not stress this enough. This alone will save you anxiety, depression and a massive amount of time and energy! Isn't the reason you became an entrepreneur because you want to do what you like doing and not all the other things?!?!

The idea of all of what we do in the grand theme of life is to get more time with loved ones. Staying happy also creates a high vibrational energy for all of us and makes ourselves more magnetic and open to great things. I prefer to be magnetic instead of chasing anything or anyone. Think about how you feel when someone is chasing you and when they are not. Which way do you feel more attracted to that person? I would say that most of us would feel less attracted to someone who we are chasing, chasing, and chasing— as opposed to creating a situation that is much more magnetic. When things are more natural, rather than forced it is more authentic.

When you're an entrepreneur you are a leader of sort, no matter how many employees you have. You are leading in your industry and people are looking to you for answers and guidance. Authentic leadership is always much more attractive than insecure levels of ego driven leadership. I believe that person who is confident and full of self-love and self-esteem is a leader that I am simply drawn to. A leader that tries too hard and works too hard—just is not that attractive to me. Therefore, not appealing for me to want to do business with.

This all brings me to my final secret. The need for continuous education and personal development growth is absolutely essential and is non-negotiable, especially for an entrepreneur. We need to stay strong and we don't have someone to tell us to go take some time off, so we have to take care of ourselves.

Personal growth never ends and therefore your education of self should never end. You should always be building up your foundation of self-worth, in order to keep it strong. Building your own tower of self-love/self worth, requires time energy and frequently money. You must set aside other things to make time for this. Your health depends upon it. If you don't invest in your health today— it will more than likely bankrupt you tomorrow.

Putting yourself first when you're an entrepreneur, is not a choice. It is absolutely 100% a must! If you somehow think or believe that you're going to just slide by that one, its not going to happen. The consequences of missing out on this, are far too high for anyone to have to pay. You will pay for sure one way or another. If you watch people who are very successful, you will see that they always make time for themselves, for their health, for their family, and for their mental and spiritual well-being! They get everything done and they are never at the end of the line.

Start making yourself a priority in your own business, your personal life as well as your love-life !! You will prosper! Thank you for letting me share just a few of my secrets in here. I know there are so many more to follow. Enjoy!

Love and Light

Marianne

~CHAPTER 2~

Finding My Purpose in Helping Others

Bill Walters

When I was growing up, car seats were non-existent. Things were just different then. That being said, my mom and I used to drive over to my uncle's salon to get our hair cut. One afternoon, while we were on our way, the rear passenger tire of my mom's car sheared off, and we lurched very hard to the right. *"Jesus!"* My mom called out as the car threw itself off the road. I remember sitting up and looking around. A man was running up to my mom's window. He had been driving his truck right behind us. I remember him telling my mom he was so glad that he was on schedule, with his route that day. He tends to speed when he runs behind and easily could have hit us.

Of course, I was young and didn't understand much of what was being said. I do remember my mom's voice frantically calling out, *"Jesus!"* before we came to a stop. I wouldn't realize until much later in life that, at that moment, we were being looked after. I went to the doctor's office shortly after that car accident, and that's when the doctor told my mother and father, that I had hip dysplasia. I was three and a half years old.

My mom always taught me to put the needs of others before my own. She always looked out for me and never put herself first. During the last 15 years that my parents were together, my dad tried to be more health-conscious and gave up sweets. So, my mom did, too, because those are the things you do for those you love. When my dad was on his deathbed, I made a promise to him that I would take care of her. She deserved it after everything she did for our family. So that's what I did.

In the years that followed, as her Dementia worsened, I took my mom on her first roller coaster, to her first Christian rock concert, and on a tour of Washington D.C., and I saw her experience swimming in the ocean for the first time. We had a bowl of ice cream together every night before bed. It was her turn to experience life's grand things, just as she always did for me. She wasn't just a wonderful mother; she was a fantastic grandmother. She would talk to my daughter and my daughter's friends about relationships, dating, and what she learned. She wished them a partnership like the one she had with their grandfather. She was never cruel or violent and never seemed to have a bad day. She was always in good spirits, even until the end.

Hospice care was the only thing that allowed me to get some rest while I was taking care of her. The last two and a half years of her life were hard on both of us. My own family did not do much to care for her or offer help when we needed it most.

She became less mobile, but she was by my side in her wheelchair everywhere I went. Everything I did, she and I did it together. For the last 36-hours of her life, she was no longer verbal and would communicate by blinking. Once for "yes" and twice for "no." She passed peacefully at 3:45 in the morning, about an hour after sending me away to get some sleep. When I talk to my clients about caring for their parents, I often talk about my mom, reminded of the love she selflessly gave to me and those around her. I tell my clients that nothing is owed to us, and we don't step up in these situations out of obligation or a contract of some kind. In most cases, we are lucky to have parents who never let us feel lonely or sidelined. The best we can do in return is to be there and let them continue experiencing life with you. Spend time by the ocean, take city tours, and eat ice cream.

There was a turning point when I discovered my passion for helping others financially. Most people think of "success" in a material sense, but I think they should think of "success" in terms of what God is calling you to do. It should be about fulfilling "his purpose" and not "your purpose" or mankind's. I wasn't a perfect dad to my daughter or a flawless caretaker to my mom, but I learned countless valuable lessons in both roles. I felt God was calling me to fulfill a higher calling and do his work and significantly impact his people by showing them the lessons I learned taking care of my daughter and mom.

I am someone who climbed the corporate ladder at a young age. Fresh out of College, I got a fancy job at a top-notch company and within a short amount of time was training my own sales team. I held a Vice President role in the organization. People looked up to me and followed me as their leader. Fancy job title, nice salary, all the material possessions I ever wanted. I achieved all these things. I had a beautiful house with a white picket fence. We took amazing family vacations and had fun.

Apparently, I was living the American Dream. But I wasn't happy or fulfilled. I was always chasing the next thing because I thought "Once I achieve this next goal, then I'll finally be happy." But that joy never came. I realized that if I am called to help or improve a situation, it doesn't matter what my job title, salary, or prestige is. I needed to help.

I felt like I was being called to fulfill God's plan, and I needed to step up and do his work and help people become a better version of themselves and improve their circumstances. People always ask me why it matters to be financially literate or financially sound. Here's what I tell them. If I could turn back the clock to my mid-20s and have better financial foundations, I could have made more sound financial decisions. I could have probably retired in my mid-40s instead of needing to work. I loaned money to family members who never paid me back, invested in fledgling businesses, bad stocks, and other poor financial decisions.

I could have saved and invested more money and achieved financial freedom. I teach simple principles that I wish someone would have taught me about budgeting, saving, not keeping up with the Joneses, getting out of debt, and living in abundance. Whatever abundance looks like for you.

Even with the amazing family I had and the awesome education I received throughout my life, financial literacy was simply never taught to me during my young adult life. I didn't realize how much it hindered me until I needed to take care of my daughter and my mom later on in my life.

There is unspeakable value in having a sound financial plan for your present and future life. The basics are rooted in trust and transparency. Many people I try to help have significant credit card debt, other family members they secretly support, and are doing things their spouse doesn't know about, etc. I teach them to bring everything to the table so we know what's happening. I show them how to create a budget for their current life and the lifestyle they want to have during retirement. We can then solve for that desired goal, develop a budget accordingly, and show them the necessary sacrifices and savings they'll need to make.

I can recall examples of clients who; spent most of their adult life saving money and making frugal financial decisions, who have lost a couple hundred-thousand dollars in the last couple of months due to things that have happened in the economy.

I, in essence, helped them place a tourniquet on the hemorrhaging of their savings. I create a unique perspective on tax free retirement not called a Roth. I do this while removing risk and tripling their savings in just ten years of time. How do I create such a plan, let's chat .

Bill Walters

Bill Walters: Financial Advisor & Founder of Perfectly Imperfect Families

Bill Walters is a compassionate financial advisor, dedicated to helping families achieve economic security and peace of mind. As the founder of Perfectly Imperfect Families, he combines professional expertise with deep personal experience to guide clients toward stable financial futures. Raised by a disciplined Navy father and a determined mother who instilled in him resilience and preparation, Bill learned early the value of hard work and responsibility. His childhood was marked by challenges, including a diagnosis of hip dysplasia that left him temporarily paralyzed and bedridden for long periods. Yet, through these struggles, he discovered perseverance—a trait that would define his personal and professional journey.

Bill's commitment to overcoming adversity continued into adulthood. After losing a track scholarship in college due to injury, he redirected his focus toward business and sales, where he embraced failure as a catalyst for growth. Later, as a father, he fought tirelessly to support his daughter through learning disabilities, health struggles, and systemic obstacles—reinforcing his belief in resilience and advocacy. A defining chapter in Bill's life was serving as the primary caregiver for his mother during her battle with Dementia.

This deeply personal experience taught him the profound importance of family, love, and planning for life's uncertainties. Today, Bill channels these lessons into his work, helping families navigate financial planning with empathy and wisdom. His approach is rooted in the understanding that true wealth lies not just in numbers but in the security to cherish life's most meaningful moments. Through Perfectly Imperfect Families, he empowers clients to build legacies of stability, strength, and love—just as his parents taught him.

When he's not advising clients, Bill enjoys sharing his insights on resilience, caregiving, and financial empowerment. He ensures that every family he works with feels seen, supported, and prepared for whatever lies ahead.

Bill Walters

www.perfectlyimperfectfamilies.com

~CHAPTER 3~

Mastery of Self Exploration

Amanda M. Renaud

Being an entrepreneur is not an easy road with band-aid solutions or quick fixes. I knew very young; money was hard to make having come from a big family. I watched my mother, a single mother of four children master business and dominate, her field quite young. She had a relentless drive and she took all her struggles and turned them into success. I mean I guess she could have let a divorce and her trying circumstances define her—but she didn't. I watched her and knew that there was more to entrepreneurship than just working hard. I knew there was a lot more to learn and understand. My journey started very young, I started working at age twelve, from paper routes to selling chocolate bars for charities—I knew it was tough.

One of the first lessons I learnt as a young woman was that hearing the word "No" did not always mean no. I learnt it truly meant you have to find another way. I knew that things will often go sideways in life and you have to find solutions and keep going no matter what. I went from being a college student and having my bills bounce regularly, to paying cash for brand new vehicles off the lot—never having to check my bank balance.

I also knew that money cant change how you feel inside. Money is merely a tool to help you in life and business. Money cant define your purpose and it cant change every circumstance—only you can do that. Having more of it wont always fix the problems and it truly is not the goal of business or life. That is an illusion about money and entrepreneurship. I had to learn that money will come and go, just like the challenges and struggles. If money is all you work for, you'll always be poor and it will never be enough. There is also a metric that we as entrepreneurs need to understand when it comes to handling challenge. We should always assess the circumstances. We assess circumstances by understanding that we can only change—what we control. Which is ourselves!!! If you do not learn this, the consequence will be that; circumstances can change you, long before you change the circumstances. What I mean by this is that; the longer you choose to ignore things and choose not to handle the challenges around you— the longer they weight in on you and your success.

It is necessary to trust yourself, your ability and avoid complacency. Leadership demands you to step outside your comfort zone but be authentic in all you do. A lack of discipline and clarity in who you are, will cause you to stumble. I see many entrepreneurs following the crowd and battling themselves, as a life coach. Hec, I was even that person once upon a time. Give up the people pleasing and follow your own path, follow the leaders who align with your journey.

Avoid the traps of doing things that are not for you, because it will burn you out quickly. Learning to manage yourself is one of the biggest struggles, when it comes to being an entrepreneur. Become the master of self discovery! It is not a 9-5 with supervisors and district managers pointing fingers and telling you what needs to be done. It is acknowledging you have the freedom to make choices that benefit you and your purpose. However, with that comes the responsibility of managing yourself and businesses. There can be limited support or cheering happening around you. Some in business, see others as competition, this is not the case. It's a myth and another illusion of entrepreneurship because your power and growth comes from networking and collaboration. It is recognizing others and what they are doing is not for comparison nor competition, but rather opportunity to learn or join! There is enough success for everyone, because success is not a pie that needs to be split up and divided, it is an unlimited serving—there's enough for everyone! It is a shared journey if you understand YOUR habits, routines, and limitations are your only competition.

An inability to recognize toxic behaviors, mindsets, patterns, and habits leads to burn out. Self-care will be one of the most important areas as an entrepreneur that you will need to focus on and regularly. You can not give to others what you do not have yourself. You can not make rational decisions when you are internally conflicted and burnt out.

Whatever makes you feel good and brings you joy, should be apart of your regular routine. Showing up for others requires you to show up for yourself first. The ability to trust yourself, cheer for yourself and show up for yourself is huge when it comes to entrepreneur secrets. You have to have the mindset that its YOU versus YOU and the barriers that keep you unproductive. Embrace the challenges, struggles, and mistakes because the compensation you will receive may not always be monetary, but rather wisdom— that will help you to meet your goals. Another vital piece of the puzzle in uncovering the secrets is...You must be goal orientated. Without goals you are simply rolling through the motions of business which leads to unfulfillment and boredom. You can not expand or have clear visions and purpose if your foundation and goals are not clear. Your goals are a roadmap to where you are going and where you want to be. Not ought to be, I say this because sometimes hard work is not enough. We all work hard, like the bees as a human species for the most part.

We can not assume that just because we are doing some parts of what needs to be done — that success will come. Success looks different for everyone, but the building blocks are typically similar. The habits, mindsets, and determination is the driving force to bring anything home. It takes a relentless drive and time. There are no overnight formulas or quick shortcuts to success, and there is no skipping steps. However, there are tools, resources, and knowledge that can make the journey easier.

ENTREPRENEUR SECRETS

Most entrepreneurs statistically do not make millions of dollars—another lie. Why? Because most give up right before the breakthrough! Any great minded individual who has contributed to todays world, did things thousands of times before finding a way that worked. The biggest secret is to have the courage to keep going! The fact that you were courageous enough to invest in yourself and create an income without relying on a 9-5 is amazing! Which brings me to my next point; CELEBRATION! There are no corporate awards or anyone holding your hand to acknowledge you or tell you that you have done well. In fact, there will be very little support or cheerleading from people around you—most do not understand the hard work. A common assumption I hear is; that they're at home working; it must be easier! It is the opposite, most entrepreneurs are working 18-hour days and juggling their families, meetings, multiple income streams, and personal care. Being an entrepreneur— there is NO CLOCKING OUT!

Being an entrepreneur can be a tough gig because it is not always easy, it comes with many different challenges. It requires regular action and maintenance. Entrepreneurs must be quick to take action and apply their innovative mindsets, with a centre focus on—solutions-based approaches. Entrepreneurs can excel when they give up the poor habits, excuses, doubt, fear and focus on lack. You can truly excel when you choose to focus on solutions and the things you already have and the things you want.

By choosing to give up the focus on lack and distractions, you can attract better and healthier elements in your everyday life. Individuals start to succeed when they are aligned with themselves, others who share the same mindset and purpose. Remain true to your vision, goals, purpose and focus on what is working during your journey. Truth is; the secrets remain buried within ourselves, only we can truly understand what it is we want, need, and are building. There will always be setbacks, challenges, and disappointments in life and in entrepreneurship. The secret is to keep going and don't stop until you are truly happy with everything you have built. Others will not understand your journey or what you're creating and they never have to! Your journey is about you and the people you serve.

Always show up with a heart engulfed by servitude and focus on your passion, the money will come. Many waste their lives chasing money, chase your passion and goals instead. Choose your own vision—skip following the crowd. Your value comes from what you have to offer, which is unique! No one can duplicate YOU! Be adaptable of course but always be authentic and your people will align with what you're doing. Master your skillsets and continue to add innovative models to your business once you have executed excellent delivery. Focus on solving your client problems and fulfilling their needs as consumers.

Everything is continually changing globally and economically, so you will have to maintain and adjust accordingly.

Sometimes easier is best rather than complicated strategies and systems—no matter what they try and sell you. Lastly, do not lose yourself in the noise of entrepreneurship, it's a very fast paced and busy life—but never give up! Entrepreneur's are needed globally, we bring the innovative ideas, strategies, and set trends in the world of business. The word NO you are going to hear a lot, but a NO is not a NEVER nor the final say— Find another way!

Lastly, believe in yourself no matter what people say and remember it can not rain forever. Remember your grace, faith, and compassion. Whatever it is you are facing is temporary, never be afraid to reach out to other entrepreneurs and ask them how they overcame their own struggles. Engage with other business owners because chances are, they have also faced similar situations. Whatever it is you refuse to change, especially when you know it is not working— you are choosing. Never let your own pride hold you back from achieving all that matters to you. You can build your own dreams or be paid to build someone else's!

Find your purpose and jump into the world of entrepreneurship, fear can never be a good leader. If you can envision it in your mind, then it can be done. The universe is always ready and willing to be your partner, its simply a matter of understanding that your journey is going to look different than others and that's your superpower. I hope you never give up and build that thing you always dreamed of. The best is yet to come!

Amanda M. Renaud

Amanda is an Experienced Leader with a demonstrated history of working in sales, leadership, and entrepreneurship for more than twenty years. Amanda is the CEO of Magnetic Publishing, founded by Robert J. Moore as Magnetic Entrepreneur. The Global Publishing Brand was featured In Forbes, Yahoo Finance and USA today. Magnetic Entrepreneur Inc also holds a Guiness World Record and won the Global Recognition award of 2023 for their continued publishing and coaching services.

Magnetic Entrepreneur Founded by Robert J. Moore a New Times Best selling Author and huge Inspiration to Amanda for many years. Amanda has rebranded into Magnetic Publishing, to add her personal touch since acquiring the business. Amanda is a 6x International Best-Selling Author herself. Amanda continues to make her impact in the publishing world, while carrying on Robert's legacy.

Amanda holds an Advanced Diploma in Child and Youth treatment and has knowledge in Program development, Community services, Crisis Intervention, Business Development, and Customer Relationship Management (CRM). Amanda is a strong professional who is also a certified life coach and has won numerous Awards in Canada for sales and her writing.

Amanda is a motor vehicle accident survivor who has made immense impact for her herself and the people around her. Amanda has transformed her life into the true definition of success. Amanda also released her first Solo Self development Novel in October of 2023 " Exceptional Minds" a wonderful prelude into her Leadership teachings and upcoming course designed to enhance leadership skills globally.

Amanda also became a number one Best Seller just recently with her newest Co-Authorship book Luminous Leaders where herself and co- authors share valuable knowledge about leadership. Amanda was presented with a lifetime achievement award recently for her continued work in publishing and contributions to leadership from the Mind Academy Arena.

Amanda continues to focus on serving others, provide quality publishing, and coaching services that are empowering the lives of many globally. Amanda is a single mother of three sons who has faced many hardships throughout her life but despite the challenges, she continues to share her knowledge and help emerging writers face the challenges in the publishing world and everyday life, with her diverse skill set and continued efforts driven by her compassion for writing and serving the people around her.

www.magnetic-publishing.ca

Magneticpublishing2023@gmail.com

~Chapter 4~

The Craziest Journey : My Life as an Entrepreneur

Maxine Willocks

Without a doubt, living the life of an entrepreneur is the most unconventional path available. There is no one straight road here. It is not for those with a weak stomach. Despite all the odds, this is the kind of road you start down with nothing in your hands but a vision in your head, a fire in your belly, and just enough persistence to think you can make it happen. People talk of starting with nothing. I started from less than ideal. I began with no money, no outside funding, and no road map—just a deep awareness that I was supposed to create something significant. I could have gone the easy route at any moment: found a 9-to-5 job, a consistent pay stub, direct deposit every two weeks, and some relief. That would have been a reasonable approach. But, if you run a business, you are aware.

Logically, this is not how things go. Vision performs. It Takes a Special Kind of Crazy Let us be honest. Entrepreneurship requires a unique kind of drive. It calls for foolishness, bravery, egoic endurance, and an unquestionable faith in something only you can see. The first few years will run every thread of your life.

The depths of not enough—not enough money, not enough time, not enough sleep, not enough support will be yours. And yet you keep on. For what? Since your fantasy keeps you from sleeping. Because you were born to create. You are chasing purpose instead of security. People who are entrepreneurs are unique. Our motivations go beyond mere financial ones. Creating drives us. Under freedom. That surge of excitement upon the first email that arrives saying, your story inspired me, or upon the purchase of your product. Every restless night is well worth it at that point.

The Adrenaline and the Exhaustion This is a busy existence. Though its exciting, its also draining. Starting Omax, I had to be everything: product development, marketer, customer service agent, sales representative, bookkeeper, and fulfilment specialist. I transported goods myself and hand-poured magnesium into jars. To pay for my next inventory load, I provided yoga sessions.

I exchanged housekeeping and cooking for web design skills. I turned every dollar I made back into the company. There were evenings when I slept nowhere. Not because I didn't want to but because I couldn't. Product formulae, marketing copy, supply chain problems, and visions of helping someone's grandmother feel better with a salve I created in her kitchen were flying through my head. Sleep turned from a necessity to a choice. Diet? Based on what I could afford. Family time is what seldom occurs.

Social life: zero. One currency I had was creativity. I lived off concepts and excitement. When I couldn't afford a developer, I produced material alone, recorded yoga videos between teaching seniors, responded to DMs at midnight, and learned how to edit Shopify code. The Highs and Lows Entrepreneurship is like riding a rollercoaster without a seatbelt. One day, you find yourself unstoppable; your social media post goes viral, or you sell out of stock. Your package gets caught at customs next, or a consumer requests a refund you cannot afford to provide. You learn to tackle problems like a cold and calculated manifesto—finding clarity among anarchy. You develop a skin so thick you can walk across fire, and occasionally, it feels like you are. This road can break you.

Ulcers are one result of it. It can bring you right on burnout. At three in the morning, you can find yourself awake thinking whether you have made a big mistake. You might not cry out but silently. You might skip vacations, birthdays, and meals. Indeed, it can cause you to withdraw. Because developing whatever only you believe in is a lonely place. Still, strangely, it is also everything.

The Pain and the Pleasure Entrepreneurship has damaged me. It has let me grow humble. But it has also raised me in ways I never would have guessed possible. Rising from ashes is something I understand. I lost practically everything following the wildfire at Fort McMurray, but I rebuilt.

Driven by a strong desire for healing and a passion for empowering others to achieve the same, I developed my brand. Omax is not only a skincare concern. My narrative fits in a jar. My grandmothers knowledge, my cultural heritage, my yoga path, my science-based wellness education, and my tenacious nature are all reflected in this. At this company, I have laughed harder than I have ever done, but I have also sobbed. I have experienced heartache— as well as a high that no career could ever provide. Like childbirth, it is agonizing, all-consuming, but finally, the most fulfilling act of creation.

The reason I keep going and I continue to do so; as someone out there needs what I am developing—the elderly arthritic person who finds relief with my balm. The woman in my account, who is recovering from burnout, is visible. The young entrepreneur listening to me, who challenges herself to dream somewhat more broadly. I continue as I think of legacy. I see healing. Achievement and self-care can coexist, and people should be shown that they can start anew. It is not easy in this life. But it is actual. For me, that is also everything.

What I've Learned

- Starting does not call for permission.

- Momentum building does not require financing.

- You learn by doing; you cannot be exceptional without experience.

- You do need grit.

- You really should guard your peace.

- Even if everything else seems uncertain, you still have to keep linked to your why.

Entrepreneurship will help you discover who you are, what you're made of, and how far you are willing to go, to achieve the life you want.

My final thoughts; If you are reading this and waiting at the brink of your leap—do it. Not for safety alone. Not even because its simple. But since your dream deserves an opportunity. More people need to have the bravery to be able to produce from nothing. Maxine Willocks here is me. I am still developing and still dreaming. I am still worn out and still fixated. And I would never swap this path for anything. Want to discover more about Omax and my goal to blend wellness, skincare, and purpose? Or follow along?

See www.omax3m.com or track me on Instagram @Omax3M.

Maxine Willocks

Maxine Willocks is a highly accomplished entrepreneur, holistic business strategist, and wellness advocate with over twenty-five years of experience building and leading award-winning businesses. From Jamaica to Fort McMurray, she has consistently demonstrated exceptional leadership, including establishing a million-dollar restaurant enterprise that garnered significant industry recognition. As a former Female Business Leader of the Year and TEDx speaker, Maxine has shared her insights on resilience and leadership in challenging environments.

Today, she seamlessly integrates holistic wellness and strategic business leadership, guiding entrepreneurs, executives, and professionals in cultivating balance, reducing stress, and enhancing performance through Kundalini yoga and mindfulness practices. Her work focuses on aligning vision with execution for sustainable success and well-being.

See www.omax3m.com or track me on Instagram @Omax3M.

~Chapter 5~

Aligned and Unstoppable: A Visionary Entrepreneur's Guide to Confidence and Clarity

Dr. Kimberley Linert

We all know an entrepreneur who looks wildly successful on the outside: a polished website, active social media, client wins, maybe even a TEDx talk or two. But behind the scenes, they're spinning. Overthinking. Second-guessing. Working harder than ever, but something feels off. If you're reading this, maybe that sounds familiar. What if I told you your problem isn't confidence, strategy, or time management? It's clarity.

Not the surface-level kind where you write out your goals in a pretty planner. I'm talking about deep, soul-level clarity—the kind that activates your nervous system, fuels meaningful action, and aligns your business with who you really are. I've spent over thirty-years as a behavioral optometrist, working with vision, brain, and body to create lasting transformation. Today, I mentor high-performing entrepreneurs to clear both their visual and mental blind spots so they can step fully into their next evolution—with purpose, certainty, and peace.

Here's what I've discovered:

Confidence without clarity is just performance. Clarity, on the other hand, builds unshakable confidence—because it's rooted in truth. Let's dive into how to tap into that kind of power.

Confidence Without Clarity Is a Trap

Entrepreneurs are often conditioned to believe that action, leads to confidence. We think, If I just do more—launch the course, redo the website, show up daily—then I'll feel ready. But that approach only works short term. It creates a performance loop: you keep doing more to prove something to yourself, but never quite feel "there." This is the trap.

One of my clients—let's call her Sarah—was a well-known coach with a multi-7-figure business. From the outside, everything looked perfect. But privately, she was exhausted and disconnected from her mission. She had built something successful—but not something sustainable or joyful. She didn't need more hustle. She needed to see herself and her future with fresh eyes. We didn't start by tweaking her business plan. We started by reconnecting her to her internal vision—what she truly wanted her life to look and feel like if she dropped all expectations and started from truth.

We used visualization, body-based integration, and decision-clarifying techniques that activated her subconscious mind.

What surfaced surprised her: she no longer wanted to grow a bigger company—she wanted to deepen her impact through more intimate, curated work. She wanted spaciousness. Grace. And joy. That inner knowing changed everything. Once her vision clicked into place, she could confidently release what no longer aligned. Within months, she created a new business model that gave her more income and far more freedom—with less output.

When you align with your true vision, confidence becomes a natural side effect—not something you chase. Without clarity, confidence becomes a costume. With clarity, it becomes your core.

Clarity Starts in the Brain (and the Eyes)

Here's something most entrepreneurs don't realize: your brain follows vision—both in the physical world and in your inner world.

Your visual system is intricately connected to your brain's attention, focus, and executive function. When your external or internal vision is blurry, your nervous system gets overwhelmed. It doesn't know what to filter out. So, everything starts to feel urgent—and nothing feels clear. That leads to mental fatigue, decision paralysis, and a constant sense of not doing enough. When you create a clear, emotionally resonant picture of where you're headed. A visual picture that engages your imagination, values, and purpose. With this, your brain can prioritize and act more decisively. This is where the science gets really exciting.

Your Reticular Activating System

(RAS) is the part of your brain responsible for filtering information and deciding what's relevant. It works like a search engine: if you tell it what to look for, it will highlight it in your environment. But if you don't program it with clarity, it just pulls up everything—and that's where chaos sets in.

Try this: **Close your eyes and imagine your business and life three- years from now.**

Where are you? Who are you working with? What does your day feel like? What lights you up?

Make it vivid. Use all your senses. Smell the ocean air if you're at the beach. Hear the voices of grateful clients. Feel the freedom in your chest as you check your calendar and smile.

Then ask yourself:

☐ What does this version of me believe?

☐ What do I no longer tolerate?

☐ What choices did I make to get here?

This isn't fluff. This is neuroscience. You're activating neural pathways that make this vision familiar, possible, and actionable. It's the same principle Olympic athletes use to mentally rehearse gold medal performances. And you can use it to run a business with inspiration, not stress.

Your brain is always asking: "What are we doing?" If you don't answer it with clarity, it will default to survival mode. There's no confidence in survival mode—only scrambling.

Aligning Vision with Strategy: The Missing Link

Clarity creates direction. But alignment makes that direction sustainable. Alignment is when your vision, beliefs, and behavior all point the same way. It's when what you see, what you say, and what you do are congruent. And in that congruence, your nervous system finds safety—and your confidence multiplies.

When I mentor clients, I walk them through a 3-part Alignment Audit:

1. Is my vision clear?

Can I see and feel the future I want in vivid detail?

2. Do I believe it's possible?

Are there subconscious blocks, limiting beliefs, or inherited fears holding me

back?

3. Are my actions aligned?

Am I making daily choices that match the person I say I'm becoming? If any of those three are out of sync, you'll feel resistance.

Let me give you a real example.

One of my clients, a brilliant health entrepreneur, came to me saying, "I want to work 20-hours a week, make $500k a year, and spend my afternoons with my kids." But when we examined her schedule, she was working 50+ hours a week, managing every detail, undercharging her services, and holding onto a belief that success required sacrifice. She didn't need more productivity hacks. She needed alignment.

Together, we rewired her beliefs around worthiness and work, restructured her offers, and created space in her nervous system to receive more by doing less. Within 60-days, she signed two ideal clients at her new premium rate—and took Fridays off completely.

Confidence doesn't require force. It flows when your system is aligned.

You're Not Stuck. You're Just Unclear.

If you feel stuck right now—spinning in self-doubt, unsure of your next move—I want you to know this: You're not broken. You're not behind. You're just not aligned yet. Most high-achieving entrepreneurs are used to pushing through. But clarity doesn't come from pushing—it comes from pausing long enough to hear what's true. What would happen if you stopped trying to be more—and instead, became more of you? That's the shift that unlocks everything.

In my work, I guide visionary entrepreneurs to:

- Reconnect with their authentic vision
- Clear internal and subconscious blind spots
- Align with their nervous system's natural pace
- And step into their next chapter with calm, confident action

It's not about becoming someone new—it's about seeing clearly so you can show up fully.

Your Next Step (Personal Invitation)

If you're outwardly successful but inwardly unsettled…

If you've built the business but haven't yet built it in a way that feels fully aligned…

If you know your next chapter is calling, but the path feels foggy…

Then I'd love to help you see it—so you can step into it.

I offer private, deeply customized mentorship for high-performing entrepreneurs ready

to:

- Clarify their inner vision
- Clear hidden obstacles from the brain, body, and belief system
- And create a life and business that feels energizing, meaningful, and fully aligned

Let's talk. Book a confidential discovery call here:

https://calendly.com/drkimberley/15min

Together, we'll uncover what's next for you—
and build the clarity and confidence to walk into
it powerfully. You don't need to do more. You
need to see more clearly. You don't need to
become someone else. You just need to become
aligned. From there, everything becomes
possible. Let's create your next evolution—from
the inside out.

— Dr. Kimberley Linert

Dr. Kimberley Linert

Dr. Kimberley Linert is a visionary mentor, behavioral optometrist, and founder of the Optic Brainfit™ method—an innovative approach that integrates vision, brain, and body to unlock human potential. With over 30-years of experience, she helps high-achieving entrepreneurs and leaders clear mental and emotional blind spots, reconnect with their inner vision, and align their lives with purpose, joy, and clarity.

Dr. Linert is also the author of *"Visualizing Happiness in Every Area of Your Life,"* host of the Incredible Life Creator podcast, and a sought-after speaker and trainer known for blending neuroscience, intuition, and transformational tools that create lasting change. She works privately with visionary entrepreneurs who are ready for their next chapter—and want to lead with confidence, authenticity, and impact.

https://linktr.ee/DrKimberleyLinert

~Chapter 6~

Unstoppable: 15 Lessons That Changed My Life and Business

Kylee Leota

Some people were born to be entrepreneurs. It's in their blood. They thrive on risk, love the thrill of the chase, and light up with ten ideas before breakfast, juggling multiple priorities with ease. That wasn't me. Or so I thought....I was born and raised to play it safe. Low risk. Stability. Get a secure job. Get married. Get a house. Stay within the lines. So, I did exactly what was expected of me—until life fell apart.

In 2014, I got so sick I couldn't hold a coffee cup. In 2015, with police support, I left a domestic violence relationship and became a single mom to three-children under age ten. That's when I realized: stability without joy is just survival — I was done just surviving. My safe government job no longer fulfilled me. But the universe wasn't done nudging me, it needed to shout— it did. I would love to tell you how I sustained an injury doing something bold and impressive, like rescuing someone from a burning building or training for a Muay Thai tournament. But no.

One morning in 2019, I simply rolled over in bed and heard a sharp crack in my neck. That was the start of a relentless, unexplainable pain journey. Seven MRIs later, and countless visits to neurosurgeons and neurologists, I was still left with no diagnosis. Just chronic pain, swelling, a severely limited range of motion, and a visual resemblance to the Hunchback of Notre Dame. It went on for months. I couldn't work. I couldn't show up in the way I used to. My career and my identity was suddenly out of reach. When a chapter closes, you want it to end on a high note, but this wasn't that.

I don't believe that everything happens for a reason, but I do believe that if we're brave enough, we can find wisdom from our wounds. Forced to stop for the first time in my life, I sat in the discomfort. I reflected, I reviewed, and I recalibrated. I stopped waiting for the *"right time."* The truth is that; that moment never arrives. There is always a reason to wait. Always a reason to play small.

Nothing changes until you decide you're done with the discomfort. That shift redefined who I was on a physical, mental, and emotional level. My identity, which had been fiercely attached to a job title and paycheck, began to unravel. During that unravelling, I stumbled across a quote that gave me the courage to lean into the unknown. Glennon Doyle, in her book **"Untamed"** said; *"My children don't need me to save them. They need to watch me save myself."*

Knife through the heart. What was I modelling to my children? That you had to stay in places that didn't serve you? That quote became my compass. I wasn't just rebuilding a career—I was rebuilding me. I didn't grow up wanting to be an entrepreneur. I did, however, always know I wanted to serve. Sometimes, life strips everything away so you can finally see clearly. I was forced to reflect. To review. To recalibrate.

Understanding the theory behind success is powerful, but theory alone doesn't change your life or your business. In my experience while coaching and consulting with leaders, entrepreneurs, and changemakers, I realized something. I realized that the single biggest determining factor in success or failure wasn't knowledge—it was a willingness to take action.

These 15 lessons are designed not just to be read, but to be reflected upon and applied. As you move through each one, use the reflection questions to pause, dig deep, and get radically honest about your own journey. Clarity without action is just potential left on the table, and you were made for more! These *"secrets"* can be accessible to everyone. As you will see, they are simple, just not easy.

Mindset & Identity (Reinvention & Inner Growth)

1. Identity is Man-Made – So Rebuild It on Your Terms

Dr. Carol Dweck's research on growth mindset proves that our beliefs directly influence our behaviours. Identity is not a fixed concept; it's a series of stories we've either inherited or chosen. Entrepreneurs who thrive are the ones who take ownership of rewriting those stories.

In life, this meant stepping away from who I was "supposed" to be. In business, it meant no longer letting my old title or background limit my future vision. In entrepreneurship, your identity shapes how you pitch, price, pivot, and persevere. Successful founders know that their inner narrative sets the ceiling on their outer impact.

Reflection Questions:

What parts of my current identity are holding me back?

Where have I unconsciously inherited stories I never chose?

What identity would I choose if I believed I could succeed?

2. Fear is the Biggest Liar – Master It Before It Masters You

Fear isn't always loud, it can be logical, disguised as procrastination, perfectionism, or over-preparation.

Neuroscientist Dr. Joseph LeDoux explains that fear responses activate before logic even gets a say. Entrepreneurs who master their fear don't eliminate it, they interrogate it. In life, fear kept me small, silent, and stuck. In business, it convinced me I wasn't ready to lead. In entrepreneurship, fear will always exist, but successful entrepreneurs move forward with it, not behind it. They use it as feedback, not a full stop.

Reflection Questions:

What is fear currently stopping me from doing?

How does fear show up in disguise for me?

What would taking bold action look like today?

3. The Speed of Your Bounce-Back Determines Your Success

According to Harvard Business Review, resilience is one of the strongest predictors of high performance. In business, setbacks are inevitable. What separates successful entrepreneurs is how quickly they recover, reflect, and refocus. There is a Japanese saying that says, *"Fall down seven times, stand up eight."* How you show up after you fall, is pivotal to how successful you are in the future. In life, this meant recovering from heartbreak and loss. In business, this meant bouncing back from rejections and pivots. In entrepreneurship, resilience is non-negotiable. Top leaders don't face less adversity; they just navigate it with more grace, speed, and skill.

Reflection Questions:

How do I typically respond to failure?

What helps me recover faster?

Who or what can support my resilience right now?

4. You Don't Need Permission – Give It to Yourself

One of the most underrated success traits is self-authority. Brené Brown's work reminds us of people-pleasing and approval-seeking behaviors that are rooted in fear and shame. Entrepreneurs who succeed at scale stop waiting for validation; they act from alignment. In life, this meant using my voice unapologetically. In business, it meant launching before I felt fully "ready." In entrepreneurship, waiting for permission is just another way that fear hides. Successful entrepreneurs become their own gatekeepers. They don't wait for the world to say yes, they go first.

Reflection Questions:

Where am I still waiting for permission?

What would trusting myself more look like?

What's one decision I can make without external validation?

5. Know Yourself to Lead Yourself

Daniel Goleman emphasises that self-awareness is the foundation of emotional intelligence, an essential trait of exceptional leaders. Entrepreneurs who succeed long-term know their triggers, energy patterns, and superpowers.

In life, this meant learning what nourished me and what depleted me. In business, it meant knowing which parts of the business to own and which parts to outsource. In entrepreneurship, clarity on your personal values and energy capacity allows you to make better strategic decisions, build stronger teams, and stay aligned even in chaos.

Reflection Questions:

What do I know about my strengths—and where am I hiding from them?

Where do I lose energy most in my business?

How can I better honour my values in daily decision-making?

6. Not All Feedback is Equal – Find Your Loving Critics

According to Amy Edmondson, psychological safety is essential for growth. Entrepreneurs don't need endless opinions; they need trusted voices that challenge with care. In life, this meant filtering out uninvited opinions. In business, it meant choosing mentors and coaches who could see blind spots.

In entrepreneurship, your inner circle matters more than your followers. Loving critics hold up the mirror without smashing it.

Reflection Questions:

Whose feedback truly helps me grow?

Who am I giving too much weight to?

How can I build a circle of trusted challenge?

7. Consistency Beats Perfection Every Time

James Clear's Atomic Habits proves that daily actions build identity and results. Entrepreneurs who succeed are not perfect—they're persistent. In life, this meant showing up even when I didn't feel like it. In business, it meant sending that email, making that call, and refining systems. In entrepreneurship, consistency is your brand's silent engine. Trust is built when people see you do the ordinary, extraordinarily well.

Reflection Questions:

What daily habits support or sabotage me?

Where am I waiting to be perfect before I begin?

What's one micro-action I can commit to consistently?

8. Ordinary Things Done Consistently Create Extraordinary Results

The British Cycling Team's strategy of marginal gains, 1% improvements, shows how small efforts compound.

In life, this looked like choosing to stretch, breathe, or journal. In business, it meant tightening processes, updating systems, and improving customer experience. In entrepreneurship, the snowball effect is real. Every micro-move builds momentum.

Reflection Questions:

What tiny habits or tweaks could improve my results?

What systems or routines need refining?

Where have I been undervaluing the power of small?

9. Learn to Fight Well – Conflict is a Leadership Skill

Amy Gallo's research shows that how we navigate conflict impacts innovation and psychological safety. Entrepreneurs who thrive know how to disagree productively. In life, this meant learning how to honour boundaries without burning bridges. In business, it meant resolving team issues with clarity and care. In entrepreneurship, constructive conflict is a superpower. Those who avoid it stifle growth. Those who master it accelerate it.

Reflection Questions:

How do I typically respond to conflict?

Where have I avoided a hard but needed conversation?

What would fighting well look like in my next challenge?

10. Micro to Macro – Vision Requires the Details

Vision without execution is hallucination. Entrepreneurs love big dreams, but the magic is in the breakdown. In life, this meant breaking my healing into one-day wins. In business, it meant translating mission into marketing, operations, and delivery. In entrepreneurship, the micro creates incremental gains, to celebrate the journey, not just the destination. Big vision dies without small, structured steps.

Reflection Questions:

What big vision have I stalled on?

What micro-steps would bring it to life?

Where do I resist the details—and why?

11. Reflect, Review, Recalibrate

Success leaves us clues.....and so does failure. But only if we pause long enough to examine them. In life, this looked like journaling, therapy, and honest self-reflection. Sit with it! In business, it can be the pre-mortem, not just the post-mortem reflection on how things went. Reflect early and often, as well as post-launch reviews, customer feedback, and strategic pivots. In entrepreneurship, reflection isn't optional; it's essential for innovation and evolution.

Reflection Questions:

What lessons have I ignored because I moved too fast?

How do I build reflection into my routines?

What part of my life or business needs recalibrating now?

12. Create Psychological Safety for Yourself First

Timothy R. Clark teaches that safety is the foundation of innovation and contribution. Entrepreneurs must first feel safe in their own identity before they create safety for others. In life, this meant allowing myself to feel, fall, and get back up. In business, it meant honouring rest, grace, and challenge. In entrepreneurship, the way you lead yourself sets the culture for how you lead others.

Reflection Questions:

Do I feel safe to fail, rest, and dream?

What practices help me return to emotional regulation?

Who helps me feel seen and challenged in healthy ways?

13. Balance is a Myth – Create Harmony Instead

Forget perfect balance. Life and business are dynamic. What matters is alignment. In life, this meant honouring seasons. Work, family, and healing. It is not an either/or, find the both/and opportunities.

In business, it meant shifting priorities while staying true to purpose. In entrepreneurship, harmony happens when your values, energy, and time all agree.

Reflection Questions:

Where am I chasing balance instead of harmony?

What needs more attention this season—and what needs less?

How can I realign my schedule to reflect my priorities?

14. Learning is a Lifelong Game

The most successful entrepreneurs never stop learning. They evolve with curiosity, not ego. In life, this meant humbling myself enough to admit I didn't know. In business, it meant embracing new technologies, marketing strategies, and delivery models. In entrepreneurship, growth requires learning what to let go of and what to lean into.

Reflection Questions:

Where am I resisting learning because of fear or fatigue?

What's one area of growth I'm excited to lean into?

How do I stay coachable?

15. Audit is Not a Dirty Word

Regular audits help you lead with intention. Whether it's energy, finances, time, or mindset, data creates direction. In life, this looked like evaluating friendships, habits, and health. In business, it meant auditing offers, ROI, and energy output. In entrepreneurship, what gets measured gets managed.

Reflection Questions:

What area of my life or business needs an audit right now?

Where am I spending energy that's no longer aligned?

How often do I review and adjust what I'm doing?

Your Next Step Isn't Massive........It's Meaningful

Entrepreneurship is a long game. It's not built on one lightning strike; it's the sum of thousands of small sparks. Your transformation won't come from one epic breakthrough. It will come from consistent, ordinary actions. This is the snowball effect. This is the power of marginal gains, just like the British Cycling Team has proven, 1% improvements add up to extraordinary outcomes. So, here's your real challenge: Don't just admire the lessons. Apply them.

Highlight what resonates. Circle the questions that sting a little. Make a plan. And more importantly, take the next best step. Nothing changes until something changes.

You are not here to be perfect. You are here to be powerful!

Now go build it, your way.

Kylee Leota

Kylee Leota is a Leadership, Behaviour and DEI Expert, and leads an international organization delivering transformational experiences for individuals, entrepreneurs, teams, and organizations seeking alignment, clarity, and growth. With over 25-years of experience in education, leadership, and behaviour change, Kylee empowers people of all ages to develop the mindset, confidence, and tools needed to live a life by design. Guided by Earl Nightingale's idea that success is "the progressive realization of a worthy goal or ideal," she helps individuals tap into their inner wisdom and turn potential into purpose.

Kylee integrates neuroscience, leadership strategy, and behavioural insight in her coaching work, collaborating with Psychologists, Psychiatrists, and other professionals to drive meaningful and lasting change. Working with clients in high-stake environments, Kylee supports values-based leadership, vision clarity, and sustainable impact.

"I'm here to walk beside you, offering guidance, encouragement, and tools as you move toward your most meaningful goals;" she says. Kylee is also the author of INFINITE Leadership and a passionate advocate for conscious leadership that ripples across lives, teams, and communities.

~Chapter 7~

Commitment to Continuity is the Backbone of Leadership

Jose Escobar

The most common way that I see entrepreneurs sabotage themselves is in the way they show up day to day. The majority of entrepreneurs that I have met are inconsistent. They are on for two weeks, then off the next. Then they are on for a month and off for the next two. When I say "off" I don't mean completely off. Rather, they are just not doing the things they should be doing daily to grow their business. As soon as someone reaches a certain level of success, apathy starts to creep in. They take their foot off the gas and slow down because it is comfortable. If you read your press clippings for too long, you will lose momentum.

Every time we lose momentum and try to regain it. It is like going up an escalator backwards, underwater. It is very, very difficult. So many people struggle with inconsistency. Leaders need to be in a state of flow consistently. They need to be fully immersed in what they do on a regular basis. You can not be a temporary leader.

Consistency is key to being a successful leader. Anybody can lead for a couple days, but consistency builds longevity. Consistency helps us weather the storms that will inevitably come. When you are getting a lot of no's, its not easy to keep showing up for sales calls. It is not easy to write a book when you feel writers block. Most people are inconsistent because it is comfortable. However, an effective leader is ready, willing, and able to step into discomfort. This requires a deeper level of discipline.

Without an outside authority imposing their expectations on them, most people lack the discipline to follow through. Too many entrepreneurs' actions are contingent upon how they feel, i.e. *"do I feel up for it today?," "am I in the mood?," "I'm tired."* I have found that the key to delivering no matter how we feel is by simply taking action rather than asking yourself how you feel. We have to act our way into feeling versus feeling our way into acting. This is never easy, but the more you choose the harder way, the more habitual it will become.

There are going to be many times that we are going to want to throw in the towel. Where were going to feel maybe we are in the water above our head. Were in too deep. Maybe were treading water indefinitely and feel like were going to drown. But a lot of times that happens when were not getting the appropriate levels of self-care. Yes, it is important that we work, work, work. Its important that we deliver, deliver, deliver, and that we are disciplined.

However, we also need to make sure that we are taking care of ourselves. Consistency also applies to self care! Consistent self care will prevent burn out and allow us to pour into others on a higher level. The reality is many of us are showing up empty to our clients and the people that we serve. We need to fill our cups. As leaders, we have to lead on all levels, including self care. And guess what, this also requires discipline! This means taking time for prayer, fitness, and journaling. It means reading books to expand your knowledge and stimulate your mind. It means creating space in your day for personal project time so you don't become stagnant in your business. It means carving out time for self reflection.

All of these are interconnected. How you do anything is how you do everything. If you're not showing up for yourself, you're not going to be able to show up well for your business. If you're not showing up well for your spouse, you're not going to be able to show up well for your business. If you're not showing up for your children, you're not going to be able to show up for your business. If you're not showing up with your health, then its a matter of time until you physically can't show up for your family or your business. They're all interconnected. You cant just forget about certain areas of your life.

As a leader, we must lead across the board. We have to lead with consistent discipline. John Maxwell says; *"leadership is influence."*

We have to be able to influence others to do what they need to do when they need to do it, whether they feel like it or not. It's easy to say what we are going to do something in the moment because we are emotionally invested, but it is another thing to execute when that emotion wears off. Leadership is an all the time thing, which is why not everybody signs up for it. And that's okay. But if you consider yourself a leader, call yourself a leader, or are perceived as a leader, then you better show up. And you better show up 100% of the time.

We have to be leaders. We have to pour into others. We have to pour into ourselves. We have to step our game up to the highest level because we are capable of it! And that's what leadership requires. As soon as you stop learning and growing and embrace comfort, guess what? Your leadership will automatically decline because it is directly linked to how you are moving the needle and sharpening the ax in your own life.

My encouragement is that we lead well, we lead all the time, and we lead with the highest level of passion, courage, perseverance, and love. If we do that, then our clients are going to be way better off. The people that we serve are going to be served at the highest level possible. That means that we are doing our job. Ultimately it means that the world will be a better place because we are fulfilling our purpose and our calling, our mission.

Jose Escobar

Jose Escobar is a 19-time bestselling author committed to empowering entrepreneurs and high-level leaders. As the founder of The Entrepreneur's Bookshelf and Connected Leaders Academy, he has organically built a 7-figure empire in just 15 months. His Connected Leaders Academy, now home to over 500 members worldwide across 47 states, 30 countries and 6 continents, fosters a dynamic network of top-performing professionals.

Through his engaging speaking presentations and transformative coaching programs, Jose has impacted over 30 million people globally. A master sales professional and devoted family man, he is happily married and the proud father of six.

Learn more about his services at **www.ConnectedLeadersAcademy.com**

~Chapter 8~
Rewrite, Fear & Rise
Stephanie Brandolini

I have been called to write this chapter for anyone who's ever struggled, or currently struggling with anxiety, self-doubt, imposter syndrome—and everything in between. Maybe you've felt fear creeping in every time you tried to step into your calling. Maybe you've wondered, Am I really capable of this? Am I enough? I know these feelings well. What I have learned and what I am here to share with you; is that rising —isn't about waiting until fear disappears. It's about moving through it, uncovering the gifts within it, and stepping forward powerfully.

But first, let me introduce myself—so we're not total strangers. My name is Stephanie Brandolini. I'm a multi-passionate writer, international bestselling author, award-winning screenwriter, and kingdom entrepreneur. Writing has always been my calling. Along the way, I discovered other gifts—leadership, coaching, and speaking my truth, in rooms I once thought I had no place in. Through my work, I help like-hearted individuals and families reawaken their passions, step into their purpose, and go after their God-given dreams.

Speaking of God—let's talk about him for a second…Throughout this chapter, I will be sharing God's role in my own journey. Let me just say, I wrestled with this for a while. I wondered if I should keep it more neutral, more universal, more "acceptable." But here's the truth: My faith is what got me here. Faith that grew into a beautiful relationship with my Heavenly Father. Faith that has given me the strength to rise, to push past my fears, and to write these words for you right now. The reason I say this and with absolute certainty, is because God saved my life.

Now, before we get into how to rewrite fear and rise, I'm being called to share my testimony…You see, over ten years ago I overcame a severe eating disorder. A prison I was trapped in for fifteen years. It consumed me, controlled me, and nearly took my life. At my darkest point, I was so underweight you could see my heart beating through my chest. There was one night—one terrifying, pivotal night—when I wasn't sure if I would wake up, the next morning.

What surprised me was that a part of me actually cared. Most of me had given up. Most of me was numb, exhausted… done with it all. Deep down, something within me still wanted to live. I now see that it was my soul—still tethered to God—crying out for help, even when my mind and body felt lost in darkness. And though I had never truly known God at that time, I still somehow knew what to do.

That night, on some kind of strange autopilot, I walked downstairs to my family's library, grabbed the Bible, and got back into bed. I clutched it to my chest, and started whispering words I had never read before, but somehow knew. *"Though I walk through the valley of the shadow of death, I will fear no evil, for Thou art with*

Me"…And OKAY, I am going to get extra real here for a second and admit that I kind of —sort of knew this verse from Coolio's infamous song. Regardless, I didn't understand what I was doing. But God did. And He answered. The next morning, my mom had me forcibly taken to the hospital, and trust me, it was not a pretty sight or experience. In fact, I was angry about it for a long time. Until I finally saw the life-saving gift that had occurred and I realized how utterly grateful I am for it. It wasn't my will that I am still here. It was God's. He saved me…For such a time as this.

So, when I say I am a woman of faith, I mean it. I am not here to push beliefs on anyone. I also can't tell my story, without telling you about the One who saved me. Maybe you use the word Universe, Source, Higher Power—and that's okay. You are welcome here. I encourage you to stay open because this is a chapter about rising. Not by ignoring fear or *"just letting it go!"* Let's be honest, that doesn't work, just by transforming it. We have better results when we start alchemizing fear into strength, doubt into certainty, and resistance into momentum.

Because here's what I believe: your struggles are not here to stop you, they're here to shape you. There is gold within the fear, the resistance, and the blocks. The very things you think are holding you back, they actually hold the key to sacred power. Sacred power within yourself, that you never even knew existed. Though many people will let fear win and never find it, I'm willing to bet you aren't one of them. If you're reading this, if you feel something stirring inside you right now, I believe you're meant to uncover the hidden gifts within your struggles. And in the pages ahead, I am going to show you how.

Let's begin.

The Pathway to Rising

After recovering from my eating disorder, there was a period of time where I was still so driven by fear, doubt, and debilitating anxiety that I honestly didn't know if there was any hope for me. I felt trapped in my own mind, stuck in cycles of overthinking and self-sabotage, wondering if I would ever break free. Fearing I was broken beyond repair. But hope was always there. Hope is a waking dream, a quiet ember that never fully dies out. In my darkest moments, with that still burning spark— there is a dream. The dream of living in freedom, creativity, wellness, and alignment with my true purpose— kept me going.

I could not always explain it, but I know now that what I was searching for, what kept me alive, was something much greater than me.

I found something beyond my own strength—
a power that catalyzed me to greater heights than
I could have ever imagined…The grace of God.
Through many struggles, trials, and failures, I
discovered something unexpected. The very
things I thought made me weak, were actually
my greatest strengths in disguise. When I
stopped resisting and instead leaned into my
challenges, while also leaning on God, I
uncovered a process—a system—that allowed
me to:

- Transform fear into fuel

- Shift doubt into clarity

- Turn resistance into momentum

- And so much more…

That system is what I'm sharing with you today.

Introducing the A.F.E.R. System

This system is designed to help you move
through fear, not around it. This isn't about
bypassing your struggles or pretending they
don't exist. This is about transforming them into
power.

Each phase builds upon the last:

- **A - Awareness & Acceptance**

- **F - Face & Look Beneath**

- **E - Embrace & Heal**

- **R - Rise in a Rebirth of Excellence**

And they all work together in a cycle of growth.

Let's begin where all transformation starts…

A - Awareness & Acceptance: The Power of Stillness

Most women I work with are already highly self-aware. They recognize when something isn't working. They can pinpoint their fears. But awareness alone isn't enough. Because awareness is uncomfortable. It's that moment when you realize you're stuck in a cycle—like a hamster on a wheel, running but going nowhere. You see the problem, but you feel trapped in it.

That discomfort?

It's actually your push forward. But first, you get to stop resisting where you are and step into Acceptance.

Acceptance: Be Still and Know

Here's where most of us get tripped up—we want to rush ahead, have our breakthroughs, and move on. I know this because I've done it. For years, I resisted stillness. I wanted to be moving, achieving, fixing, breaking free. I didn't want to sit with the discomfort of where I was. Every time I rushed ahead, I missed something crucial. This is Because true growth happens when we pause. *"Be still and know that I am God "*is a verse that's helped me immensely through this.

Stillness is not passive—it's an active choice to surrender. It's trusting that even in the fear, even in the struggle—you are exactly where you're meant to be, and most importantly, God is with you.

There's a vital tool to finding acceptance by the way, a simple one we use everyday without even thinking about it. That tool is breathing. Accepting what you've been afraid to see in yourself can be overwhelming, triggering anxiety to take over. When this happens we often forget to breathe. Our thoughts race, our bodies tense, and we disconnect from ourselves. So, let's breathe and reset.

Seven is a spiritual number—symbolizing completion, alignment, and divine rest. So, let's use seven-count breathing to bring stillness and presence into this moment.

1. Breathe in for 7 seconds.

2. Hold for 7 seconds.

3. Exhale for 7 seconds.

Do this for three rounds.

Feel the shift.

No need to fix anything. Just be here. When you allow yourself to fully accept this moment, fear begins to lose its grip. And in this stillness, God meets you.

F - Face & Look Beneath: Meet Yourself and Uncover the Wound

This is where things get interesting. You've accepted that this fear exists—and now, it's time to face it. This is where stillness will help you immensely because most of you will want to run. Fear has a way of triggering that fight-or-flight response—the urge to distract yourself, move on, push it away, or freeze.

However, God didn't give you a spirit of fear, but of power, love, and a sound mind. So instead of running, I encourage you to stay. Close your eyes. Look at this fear in your mind's eye. If your thoughts start racing, bring back your breath. Breathe in for seven, hold for seven, exhale for seven. Let that stillness settle in. And when you're ready, look beneath it. Fear is rarely about what we think it is. The things we think we fear most—rejection, failure, not being enough—is usually a reflection of something deeper.

A part of us that was wounded long ago.

A part of us that never fully healed.

And that wound?

That's where God is waiting to meet you. If you stay in stillness long enough, you'll begin to sense the part of you that's reacting to this fear you're facing. When I have done this, I have often found a child-like version of myself. Let's be real—sometimes, she's throwing a tantrum. You know the one. The part of you that's screaming, *"This isn't fair! or I can't do this"!* Yeah, that's her. But instead of silencing her, listen. Instead of dismissing her, see her. Instead of running away, stay. Keep looking beneath. Beneath, beneath, beneath. Until that part of you—the scared, fragile, younger version of yourself—stands still enough to face you too.

That's when the real work begins.

E - Embrace & Heal: The Power of Compassion

Now, embrace her. The part of you that has been afraid. The part that has carried the weight of this fear for so long. Accept her fully. In your mind's eye, visualize embracing her. She might struggle at first. She might not trust that you're really here for her. Hug her anyway. And as you do, imagine God embracing you both.

You are mine and he would whisper; "*I have always been with you.*" Visualize any burden she has been carrying—falling away.

Like debris that no longer serves. Like a shroud of shadows, she has outgrown.

Watch it fall away.

And what remains?

Just her.

Whole. Seen. Loved.

Let her come into stillness with you. It might take time but when she does, she will hug you back. And in this moment, healing begins. This step is rarely a one-time fix. If you're anything like me, you may have suppressed this part of yourself for years. Maybe she's afraid you'll do it again. So, trust must be built. Come back as many times as you need.

Hold her. Speak to her. Let her know that this time, you're not going anywhere. Because the more you embrace her, the more whole you will become.

R - Rise in a Rebirth of Excellence

Now, you are ready to rise. You can only rise with her. The part of you that carried the wound—she is your key. Because within the wound she carried lies the very gift that was meant to be found. Think of an oyster. The grit, the irritation—it's all been there, shaping something precious.

Now, the pearl is ready.

And so are you.

As you embrace her, feel her merging with you. Not separate. Not something you need to "fix" or "manage." But part of you. Let her dissolve into you, like mist absorbed by light. Because she is no longer your wound—she is your power.

And together, you rise.

Not just in strength, but in faith.

Not just in confidence, but in divine identity.

Not just in success, but in the purpose God has ordained for you.

Final Reflection: Your Rising Moment

Take a moment to write (or voice record) the answer to this:

• What gift did I find within my wound?

• How does it feel to rise with this part of me, instead of against it?

Let the words flow freely.

There is no right way to rise—only your way.

But know this:

You were never broken.

You were never lacking.

You were always meant to rise.

And now?

You have.

Closing: Your Rise is Just the Beginning

What you've just experienced is a brief introduction to the A.F.E.R. System—a process that goes far deeper in the full program. This is not just a transformation. It's a way of being. You are meant to rise—again and again. I would love to hear how this process went for you, feel free to connect with me via social media or the link in my bio. If you're ready to deepen this journey and rise even higher, let me know.

Because your dreams are waiting. And so is God.

With love,

Steph Brandolini

Stephanie Brandolini

Stephanie Brandolini is a international best-selling author, award-winning screenwriter, speaker, and faith-led creative visionary based in Vancouver, Canada. After graduating from film school, she rose through the visual effects industry, gaining firsthand experience in TV and film production. But through a series of refining trials, Steph was drawn into a deeper calling—to lay down striving and surrender her gifts fully to God.

Now, as a creative Kingdom entrepreneur, Steph is on a mission to glorify God through story and screen. She empowers purpose-driven individuals and families to rise in faith, reclaim their health, break free from the systems that drain them, and build time-rich, legacy-driven lives. Whether she's writing, speaking, mentoring, or creating transformational media, Steph leads with obedience, vision, and bold creativity—all for the glory of God.

Connect with Steph:
www.stephaniebrandolini.com

~Chapter 9~

Your Story Is the Strategy

Karen Hewitt

The biggest secret to being a successful entrepreneur isn't a formula or a system. Can those be learned, copied, and followed with a step-by-step process? Yes! This means that if formulas and systems were the secret sauce, everyone would be winning, making the top 1% no longer the top 1%, but rather the top 100%. Now, I know we wish this would be the case, but it sometimes doesn't work that way. Systems, formulas, and patterns are easily replicable; the reason why people do not use these, is the time portion. It gets pushed off to later when I am successful or need the system. So, I challenge you to think about what the secret could be, if not some program, funnel, system, or formula. Think about this.

Why are the messy, quiet, overlooked parts of your life your most powerful business asset? Why does everyone think that they need the glow-up? The hyped-up underdog story. You know the story I am speaking of. The before-and-after. The six figures from my laptop in Bali story. All day at the beach, nights at 5-star restaurants, and beautifully curated aesthetics. The perfectly polished origin tale that makes it all look inevitable.

ENTREPRENEUR SECRETS

What if I told you that the most powerful
tool in your business isn't that funnel, a filter, or
a formula? You can learn each of these by
following step-by-step instructions. Its your ugly
story. The one you almost deleted from your
memory. The one where you were googling how
to start a business with no money at 3 AM while
your baby cried and your brain whispered,
you're not cut out for this. You cant do this.
You're not enough. The moment when you feel
like you didn't have an option. The moment you
felt that all you were destined to do was wake up,
work, come home, sleep, then repeat. There it is!
Because the truth is, people don't buy perfection.
They buy resonance. Your most resonant content
wont come from looking put together. It will
come from telling the truth. The messy,
unfiltered, human truth. This is where your
power lives. Your entrepreneurial power!

The Lie of the Perfect Origin Story

Lets debunk this really quick. You do not
need to have survived trauma or built an empire
by thirty, to have a story that matters. Some of
the most powerful shifts I've had, personally and
professionally, came in these little moments that
would never go viral, the ones that, if you didn't
think about it, you would miss. Such as when I
realized I was burnt out and still pretending I
wasn't. Or when I chose to rebuild after betrayal,
with no hype, no spotlight, just grit. Or when
someone told me I was too emotional to be taken
seriously, I decided that my emotion, was my
edge.

These weren't the flashy moments that we usually write about. But they were foundational. Still, most of us try to write ourselves out of our story. We dilute it. We believe we should only focus on the significant aspects. We chase aesthetics. We imitate people who look like they've figured it all out, hoping well to get the same results if we copy the captions, branding, and energy. But mimicry is a trauma response. Its fear in a fancy outfit. What your audience wants isn't a carbon copy of someone else's success story. They want to see you in process, in progress, in your power. They want to see themselves in you and see how they have potential. This is what happens when you stop performing and start telling the truth.

The Secret Sauce: Your Mess Is the Message (and the Structure)

Want to know what works in content? Does that work to drive success? Its not the algorithm hacks. Its not the curated grid. Its not the hype reels. Its when someone sees your post and thinks, Oh wow... I thought it was just me. That is emotional safety. And safety is what sells now. We are in an age where your audience is skeptical, overstimulated, and tired of being sold to. They don't want to be polished. They want proof.

Proof that you've been where they are.

Proof that you're still human.

Proof that this isn't just a highlight reel with a checkout link.

Thats why your story isn't just marketing; its medicine. Its healing. Its proof. But here's where it becomes strategy:

The 7:2:1 Framework - Reimagined Through Story

Instead of pushing your offer every post, try building structure through connection: 7 parts story connection. Talk about the hard moment. The ordinary moment. The in-between. Show them who you are without the pitch. Your UGLY truth. This is where trust forms. 2 parts soft service. Gently share your offer. Don't sell, serve. Frame your product or program as a solution you built from your own experience. These posts say: I created this for the version of me who used to be you. 1-part direct CTA.

Now that they trust you, you invite them to buy. With confidence. With clarity. With love. This rhythm doesn't just convert. It builds community. When people feel seen, they do not just follow you; they stay. Your story, layered through this rhythm, becomes more than content. It becomes structure.

Your funnel becomes familiar.

Your pitch becomes permission.

You stop sounding like a salesperson.

And you start sounding like someone worth walking with. Stop Copying. Start Unmuting. Lets go there. You cant build a movement while speaking in someone else's voice. You cant lead from behind a filter.

Also, you definitely cant copy someone else's captions, energy, or tone and expect to feel fulfilled. It doesn't work. Not long-term. Because of your real edge? Its your story. You may have lived things most people wouldn't survive. More than that, you have dealt with situations where you had the opportunity to stop, to give up, and then you kept going. This is where you show that others can keep going, too. Youve healed in places most people would still be hiding. Youve risen from things you don't even post about, and somehow, you still doubt your ability to lead.

That imposter syndrome sneaks in! Yet that's precisely why you are. You don't need to perform empowerment. You are empowered. You don't need to chase credibility. You embody it. All that's left is to unmute your magic.

Show up.

With your real words.

Your real story.

Your real strategy.

Because you cant outsource your voice.

You cant delegate your lived experience.

That is your intellectual property.

That is your brand foundation.

And that is the thing no one else can duplicate.

Your Story Is the Community

The biggest lie you've been sold is that your story is just for content.

Its not.

Its for connection.

Its for leadership.

Its for community-building.

Its the spark that turns followers into family, customers into collaborators, and posts into movements. When you share your story, the messy one, the honest one, even the ;I'm still figuring this out one, you give people permission to stop pretending.

You create safety.

You model courage.

You invite real engagement.

Not clicks.

Not claps.

Commitment.

Thats the kind of business intimacy were building now. When you post your story using the 7:2:1 flow, its not just about sales psychology and impact; its about soul alignment. Its about letting people meet you before they buy from you. Its about building belonging before you build your bank account. And guess what? When they belong, they buy. When they feel safe, they stay. When they trust you, they tell their friends. This is how you scale without selling out.

This is how you lead without burning out. This is how your story becomes your strategy, and your structure.

Quick Ideas to Help You Start Sharing Today. Try posting the story about one of these this week and watch what shifts:

- There was a time when I thought I had to fake it to make it. This is what I've learned
- since...
- The hardest moment in my business didn't look like a failure; it looked like staying
- silent.
- I created this offer because I remember what it felt like to need it and not have it.
- This part of my story didn't go viral, but it changed everything.

Final Word

You don't need a perfect Insta-life to be powerful. You don't need a polished story to be profitable. You just need to be honest and brave enough to tell the truth. Not the marketable truth. The real one. The one that says: I've struggled. I've failed. I've rebuilt— and I'm still here. Still here leading with heart, strategy, and soul. That is who people want to follow. That is who they will remember. That is who builds a legacy. So, tell the story. Show them how you got to your ending, even its just your middle right now. Not because its perfect. Because its yours and someone out there is waiting to see themselves in it

Karen Hewitt

Karen Hewitt is a Harvard-Certified Disruptive Strategist, unapologetic social media strategist, and network marketing mentor for rebels who refuse to shrink to fit. A neurodivergent mom of five and the force behind Blossom to Success, Karen helps overlooked creators turn their messy, unfiltered stories into movements, income, and freedom, on their own terms.

Known for blending systems, soul, and strategy, Karen teaches entrepreneurs how to unmute their magic, build community-first businesses, and turn the ugly parts of their past into the most profitable part of their brand. Her mission? Prove that you don't need to hustle yourself into burnout to build an empire that feels as good as it looks.

Contact links

www.BlossomToSuccess.com

or

Karen@Blossomtosuccess.com

~Chapter 10~
The You ECONOMY
Tammy Williams

Secrets of an entrepreneur what a thought! You know, I have never put pen to paper on what some of my secrets that keep me grounded with conviction— are until this point. I have written down many things about why I like being an entrepreneur, what it takes to be an entrepreneur and the reason why I wanted to be an entrepreneur. However never thought about the secrets that fuel me. I am so I'm ecstatic to be able to share a few.

We all know that kid-boy or girl who had the lemonade stand, he/she used to knock on peoples doors asking if they needed their driveway or their walkway shoveled, leaves raked or even picked blueberries, sold them, offered babysitting service, and delivered the newspapers. They did it through the rain, through the sleet, the snow, and heat. This is interesting because some of those kids, I believe, are some of us entrepreneurs with drive and are goal-oriented individuals.

I feel like I'm having a conversation with myself and I'm so glad you are here with me. When I think of it there are many secrets of an entrepreneur.

Some are very common amongst entrepreneurs like discipline, focus, resilience, and risk taker etc. I believe there are some core secrets that we all seem to have. Allow me to share a few of mine.

Having confidence

To start off with, I would like to say that entrepreneurs have this confidence that they can accomplish what they set out to do. For me part of my confidence came from passion, a dream of being my own boss. Picking who I wanted to work with and even firing clients. My confidence developed from me being a sales associate for a variety of industries. For years as an employee, I made my employers hundreds of thousands of dollars. I trained and supervised sales staff. I received a mere drop in the bucket in compensation for my skills. I was not only a wife also a mom of three and I was time broke.

Although I needed a steady income, I finally mustered up enough courage and confidence that had me thinking about how I could use my skills to buy my time back and monetize on my skills as an entrepreneur. This confidence turned into belief in myself. Belief that what I have is of value. Heck, I had been paid as an employee for years for it. It also came from a space of knowing some price offers as a sales associate were inflated. I knew I could offer the same or better service and get results for clients a lesser fee. Not to compete but to serve! Serve in space where some offers are simply overpriced, plus it aligned me with wanting to help others.

Taking care of myself and prioritizing my time

Some things that have allowed me to stay on point daily is as simple as adding more fun into my life; colouring, daily walks, drinking lots of water, getting an adequate number of hours of sleep, eating less processed foods, taking the right supplements, and so much more. Although time and money freedom are included in my goals, I realize that without optimal health, nothing can get accomplished. I have met and worked with some top entrepreneur professionals crushing their business goals but ignoring their health goals. After a regular check up discovered that I was anemic and needed a blood transfusion. They recommended adding taking care of myself to my goals list, the reason for taking care of myself is in my top four. I realized not paying attention to the food I was eating, along with literally getting four- hours of sleep a night was not sufficient. I was sleep deprived because I was researching or having zoom meetings with people all over the world. This had to change.

Naturally prioritizing my time is paramount as a mom of three, wife, and a cheerleader of many. I had to get comfortable with saying no. Sometimes it means not attending everything I get invited to and not making someone's urgency my emergency. Realizing that I don't have to do it alone. My original thinking as an entrepreneur, I would be doing everything. It didn't take me long to realize the things that I didn't know how to do.

Putting a business plan together highlighted the many things I didn't know how to do or even like doing. I recall my mom telling me in my twenties while as was an employee, to buy my weaknesses and sell my strengths. I didn't understand it then, but in my later years of struggling to do it all by myself, it finally sank in. I would need a team of people to turn my goals into accomplishments. So, I began developing relationships and looking for individuals who were great at the administrative tasks. I began to fully understand and develop a fondness towards networking, where I met like-minded individuals. These individuals provided support, collaborated with me and I even learned of new opportunities. I had to learn to rely on and trust those working with me to get it done. Some of the entrepreneurs I admired had only shared their successes, never mentioning that a team was behind them.

The notion that we have to be great at everything is very misleading. I understand more than ever that no one can do it alone. Mindset is everything. I believe that at a young age, I had a positive mindset, when things went wrong or didn't go as planned. For me, it was not making the junior basketball team the first year that I tried out, only to make the grade 9 team. I was chosen to be the Centre. That is probably where I learnt to never give up. Learning that being relentless, in pursuit of my goals was necessary to succeed.

This type of mindset only increased, as I became interested in self-improvement, growing, and realizing that learning must be continuous. Staying focused on my goals, ignoring all of the nay sayers who questioned; "why I would keep calling a company that had been in the sales database for 7- years. They hadn't become a client prior to me joining the company, only after seven months I was able to offer the right solutions which garnered a signed $45k advertising plan. Then with our first property flip, we bought a 2-bedroom with a finished basement, unpaved driveway, walking distance to the lake, and many tried to discourage us from buying it, because it was a 2- bedroom, and not a 3-bedroom. Only to have a lady who was downsizing buy it. When we drown out the noise, the mindset of an entrepreneur is unshakeable, resilient, and they view setbacks as a learning experiences. We are not limited by others limited beliefs.

You could literally go into entrepreneurship by turning something you love doing or the particular skill set that you are or have been paid to do as an employee. Going into entrepreneurship for the money rewards, is not a good reason to join this profession. It really should be about serving others and being of value, all of the rewards will follow. Acquiring any of these traits is not limited to entrepreneurship; it can be helpful your job or all areas of life.

In conclusion, we have to be accountable and take responsibility for our endeavors, because all of the teachers, mentors, and personal trainers wont make us smarter, wealthy, or physically fit. A millionaire once said: *"People do bot have the patience to dedicate three-years to building their own business, but they have patience to work for others for 40-years."*

Tammy Williams

Tammy Williams

Tammy Williams is a wife, mom of three, still makes her husbands lunch, a 5x International Best-Selling Author, and Entrepreneur with over 15 -years in marketing and sales. She has a passion for helping break the inequalities that women have been faced with a for centuries, hence her collaboration as an Advisory Board Member For Camera's For Girl's, a registered Charity. Also, an Advisory Member for International Men's Day Canada. The Founder of Women, Champagne, and Real Estate and CryptoSmart Chicks.

A firm believer that your health is wealth has led to being a Health Advocate with APLGO and worked in the Diabetes and Auyervada Health sectors. She also believes we all can give and she started a Walk a Mile in her shoes campaign, several years ago and has been able to collect over 400 pairs of ladies new and gently worn footwear. This footwear which has been donated to various places in Durham region.

Tammy Williams

www.womenchampagneandrealestate.com

She can be found on social media

Facebook Women,Champagne and Realestate

~Chapter 11~

What Does it Mean to be an Entrepreneur and Why Would I Wish to B11e One?

Josef Stetter

What does it mean to be an entrepreneur and why would I wish to be one? Being an entrepreneur simply means you are doing something that creates you extra revenue and fuels your enthusiasm; it does not entail operating a fortune 100 corporation immediately. Which paradoxically drives most individuals away from ever even attempting. Many entrepreneurs battle initially, so having mentors, a tribe or mastermind to assist you and help view things from several perspectives is very crucial. A mentor and a mastermind both provide ideas you might not consider on your own. They provide connections to individuals who could become clients, vendors, suppliers, strategic partners in helping to raise and expand your company more quickly and easily.

More than ever, there are countless possibilities. Todays people can generate a consistent income and work from home, with as little as a computer and an internet connection.

Among the side hustles are: voice over, tutoring, teaching (music, art, crafts, video game playing, programming, cooking and many more), translation, writing and editing, animation, video editing, graphic design, content production on social media, drop shipping, and playing video games.

Two excellent websites to observe

how other people profit from their brilliance are **https://www.fiverr.com/ and**

https://www.upwork.com/. Therefore, one can hope that it is obvious that possibilities abound all around!

The reality is that there is NO job security left! The epidemic demonstrated this as 65-million North Americans lost their employment. Many of us understand the need of having a backup strategy, or a side gig, which might turn a greater revenue than your usual 9 to 5. A prudent approach is to get a job and to fund your passion. This will help you to acquire knowledge and expertise. Choose something you like, rather than just a decent paying career. Should you see a trend? JOB means Just obey your employer, or journey of the broke—or just over broke if you were never informed. While a career is pursuing a love, a job is pursuing money. Mark Twain once remarked; *"Find a job you enjoy doing, and you will never have to work a day in your life."*

ENTREPRENEUR SECRETS

Being an entrepreneur is having the freedom of choice and time in ones life. In contemporary society, it has developed to signify far more than merely a means of income. Talking about an entrepreneur, is talking about someone who is inventive and clever enough to see a market void. It is also seeing the chance it offers.

Entrepreneurship is open to everyone. Whether they are young or old, educated, or uneducated, they come from all backgrounds. Their distinct traits are uniqueness, creativity, and a strong will to succeed. Although there are advantages to working alone, becoming an entrepreneur does not require it. One person can not live on this earth alone. We can not do it, therefore let us say we need one another's help. Everyone is subject to this rule. If you run a company, a partnership, or a sole ownership, whoever do you depend on? Clients!

Though your company is tiny enough that you can run it alone, you still require the assistance of others. The great thing is that no matter what you want to provide, its important that it improves, invents, or delivers something fresh. You can be guaranteed there is a market for it and people all across the world that will purchase it. Being an entrepreneur, therefore allows you more freedom and choice; particularly when you have resolved the kinks and discovered what is required to expand the company.

Having a job, that you love and that pays the bills as well as funds your aspirations is important. It means you need to obtain the best of both worlds, and don't stop until you do

Now let us investigate what is the appropriate company for you alternatively known as your WHY. Your why is that one or two things that thrills you, that inspires you or that gives you a purpose broader. For some it is their family or the chance to provide them a better life and generational wealth. For others it is increasing awareness and resources for a particular problem or cause such an illness.

Some are motivated to improve the world by leaving a legacy and influencing it. A "WHY" can be to improve the environment; a why can be to honour someone who has passed, suffered, or benefited from you in their life. There is no single WHY or correct WHY. Rather, there is the one or two that inspire life and enthusiasm in you.

HINT: The money is not the WHY but rather, it is what you can accomplish and who you can assist with the money. It is, in other words, the outcome of affecting people and creating change. **HINT:** Your WHY grows the more you can help others, and as a business owner you will have more chances.

These exercises could assist you in identifying your why:

One hundred lists. In five minutes, a timer will sound; you will have to do this task as fast as you can. This is supposed to be a free-flowing mental exercise.

Your lists topic is yours to choose. Here are some lists you can make:

➢ One hundred things I want to do in my lifetime
➢ One hundred things I wish I hadn't said or done
➢ One hundred people I want to reconnect with
➢ One hundred things I would do if I had an endless supply of money
➢ One hundred things I like
➢ One hundred things I dislike

…………and so on and so forth. Though you decide, I would advise addressing a broad spectrum of options. Including the same items twice on your list is OKAY. Two of my best friends and I, participated in this event together and then exchanged notes. The results were, to say the least, surprising. Once you cross the 50th position and enter the final 50, you will begin to notice reoccurring motifs. Even if you say the ideas in various ways and use different words, there will be a prevailing tendency (or two) you repeat mentioning.

Using the most regularly cited aspects from your list, construct a fast summary. As you find your why, this will enable you to know more who you are and what you are about. Imagining yourself unearthing a time capsule buried by your family in the backyard of your childhood house is another excellent activity.

Time has passed, so you forget what was in the hidden compartment. You find a letter from your younger self as a present. Young you is only curious about how things turned out for you today, specifically, where you are, how you arrived here, and what decisions you took that brought you here. Respond to your own letter. This letter-writing prompt lets you reach out to someone from your past or present. Its healing qualities are remarkable. This article is for you if you are struggling to let go of the past, perhaps as a result of a relationship that ended unexpectedly, that has left you bewildered and longing for an explanation. Maybe you can not find one since the other person is no longer in your life. They may have moved on, but reaching out to them is still a poor choice. Why not attempt writing?

The writer might be either asking or answering the questions. Since this communication is meant only for your eyes, ask whatever you want; nothing is off limits. You will see trends in what your letters indicate requires response. They will get you closer to your Why.

The third activity is to discover your why: Write your own obituary or death note. We know the value of writing a Will. Many people view it as duty to make things simpler for their loved ones upon death. Writing your obituary also lends itself to a similar argument.

Anyone who has been given this duty will agree that writing an obituary for a loved one is not simple. As a present to your loved ones, I urge you to write your own personal farewell letter. Tell me how it sounds. How happy are you with your achievements? Is writing even one paragraph hard for you? Should this be true, write the eulogy of your fantasies. Don't hold back; think big and take chances. But you have to be honest. My friend, how do you want to be remembered? Here is the possible basis for a radical transformation to occur. It is also ingrained in there. Knowing your Why, what will you do with that information? Should you have completed the exercises, you will be able to find your Why. It might be a [blank], so that [blank] statement, but its not essential. A single word, a phrase, a sentence, or perhaps a full paragraph could all help you to respond to this inquiry.

What motivated you to seek your Why? Since we mean to benefit from it. Reaching out to your personal Why is absolutely necessary for reaching your personal best. Simply be, breathe deeply, and let your Why lead you. The moment has come to begin the transition. Everyone is mutable, contrary to popular opinion. All we can count on is that events will evolve. Things are continually changing; hence you might have to update your Why statement with time.

Still, I believe your first Why statement is the one that most accurately describes your core identity and will guide you through the numerous obstacles that change constantly presents. Living the most purposeful life is doing what you love since it matters!

Its totally your call. Either get out there and start living or hang around on the side lines and accept a lousy life. Sadly, 80 to 90% of North Americans HATE their employment. Most individuals despise what they do and NEVER alter it since they are too terrified—consider that. we all require you! Please remain among the living. Find your Why, and you will experience the uninhibited delight, that results from assisting others.

So, who am I to give this counsel? Josef Stetter is my name; I had to change jobs over 18X and professions nine times in order to find my purpose and my passion for business. Along the road, I began assisting individuals find their ideal careers now and also businesses to recruit the appropriate fit individuals and retain them for their firms.

Every time I have a chance to offer my knowledge on job searching, career Changes and corporate culture I light up with enthusiasm. So far, I have assisted more than 11,000 individuals, some in as little as two days. This is part of my why, to assist more than a million individuals find their ideal employment right now.

My lovely children and wife who motivate me, support me, and constantly make me laugh are the other half of my why. I had a business partner who taught me a life lessons that set me back over $330,000 and nearly ten years off course of my passion and purpose.

Until I met my amazing wife, I was unhappy and confused, I stopped allowing my light to shine and wanting to be an entrepreneur who wanted to improve the world. I discovered the correct masterminds and mentors; presently I am broadening my interests in several entrepreneurial prospects. This because I can assist additional people and demonstrate to my family that everything is feasible. That is why I developed a program providing all the tools, resources, processes, and techniques people need to assist all job searchers, get employed more quickly and easily.

www.landyourdreamjobnow.com

Should you require assistance in hiring the appropriate individuals for your business and improving the corporate culture, contact the Celebrate Group.

~Josef Stetter~

For over 16 years, Josef Stetter has incorporated humour, energy, passion, and full self-expression into his personal and professional life.

☐ Award Winning & International Best-Selling Author of Canada Congratulations you are hired: It was easier than you thought & USA Congratulations you are hired: It was easier than you thought. Published four other books. ☐ Award winning Speaker and Guinness World Record Participant

☐ Didn't know what I want to do when I grow up so switched careers 9 X and jobs 17 times

☐ Work in Recruitment. Clients have included: Deloitte & Touche, Aecon Construction, Tata Consulting Services, Canon, Aviva, Skechers Shoes and more!

☐ Personally, helped over 12,000 find a job they love with a 90% success rate of finding anyone employment in any field in under 3- months with proven systems. Fastest helped people land a great role is 2 days.

☐ Josef Stetter brings forth an interesting twist to getting things done and achieving results that go well beyond expectations.

☐ Josef Stetter helps you take the headache out of navigating the abyss of job searching or hiring by sharing advanced strategies that maximize results.

He understands the importance of clear, concise, confident, and conversational communication to generate results that are truly unbelievable!!!

About Land your Dream Job

I understand the job market very well, while connecting people to their purpose and identifying the right opportunities —whether advertised on a job board or knowing what's going on inside the hidden job market. I changed careers nine times and had a multitude of jobs so I understand your frustration when it comes to proving your transferable skills. Invested 25,000 to master the psychology of job finding and have systems and tools that Guarantee Results

As a career coach and job market advisor for two decades, I've written several books on the subject matter, have assisted thousands of people land their dream job and continue to support people with valuable resources and tools.

This program is definitely for you if you're feeling:

· Anxious from job loss due to Covid-19

· Frustrated with the lack of response to your job applications

· Overqualified

· Frustrated that you haven't gotten the job you really want

· Unhappy with your current employer

· Ready for a career change

The Land Your dream job program has 8 Modules plus bonus modules. There is a pre-recorded Video and Audio, there is a PowerPoint slide deck for each unit, there is also PDF files of resources that includes templates, research on where to network, top agencies in Canada and USA, explaining the psychology of interviewing, questions candidates can ask interviewer, top job finding sites and more.

These are some of the useful tips and tools you will learn from my program:

1. Secrets about the Applicant Tracking System and how the algorithms score your resume Getting responses from online applications

2. RESUMES that get noticed

3. How to WOW the interviewer

4. Optimizing Your Job Search – LinkedIn, Networking & Referrals

5. Creative job finding strategies

6. Working with recruiters/agencies and getting interviews

7. Salary negotiations

8. Creating a position just for you that does not exist

AND SO MANY BONUSES!!

https://www.linkedin.com/in/josefstetter

Gmail: landyourdreamjobnow@gmail.com

About the Celebrate Group

We at The Celebrate Group understand corporate culture and the importance of team unity, thus we become part of your team as Corporate Culturalists, providing clear and creative solutions to excite and engage your staff, thereby increasing your company productivity by a minimum of 25%. We promote the right kind of corporate culture by increasing hiring efficiencies when we find the right candidates, at the right time, using an in-depth analysis, understanding of skills required while leveraging vast networks, both online and offline. We combine our sourcing strategies with high-level psychological, personality and value assessments to ensure the highest level of compatibility between the company, as well as the candidates' needs. Let's start the conversation and see the possibilities unfold!

www.thecelebrategroup.com

~ Chapter 12~

Overcoming Fear to Unleash Your Entrepreneurial Potential

Tuesday Goodson

The entrepreneurial journey is often romanticized as a path paved with innovation, freedom, and boundless success. While these elements are certainly attainable, the reality for many aspiring and even established business owners is a constant battle with a more insidious foe: fear. It lurks in the shadows of every bold idea, every calculated risk, and every necessary leap of faith. For countless individuals, this fear isn't just a fleeting emotion; it becomes a crippling force, preventing them from taking the first step, from scaling new heights, or even from continuing down the path they've already begun.

This chapter delves into the pervasive nature of fear in entrepreneurship, how it manifests, and, most importantly, provides actionable strategies to overcome it, transforming it from a roadblock into a stepping-stone towards your ultimate success.

The Anatomy of Entrepreneurial Fear

Fear isn't a monolithic entity; it presents itself in many forms, each with its unique paralyzing effect. Understanding these different facets is the first step toward dismantling their power over you.

Fear of Failure

Perhaps the most common and potent fear. The dread of investing time, money, and emotional capital into a venture only for it to collapse can be overwhelming. This fear often stems from societal pressures, personal expectations, and the misconception that failure is an end, rather than a learning opportunity. It can lead to analysis paralysis, where an entrepreneur endlessly researches and plans but never executes, or to procrastination, delaying crucial decisions and actions.

Fear of Success

While seemingly counterintuitive, the fear of success is very real. It can manifest in the form of anxiety about increased responsibility, public scrutiny, the need to maintain performance, or even the feeling of not being worthy of such achievement. This fear can lead to self-sabotage, where an entrepreneur unconsciously undermines their own progress as they approach a significant breakthrough, or a refusal to scale up, keeping their business small and manageable to avoid the pressures that come with growth.

ENTREPRENEUR SECRETS

Fear of Judgment and Criticism

Launching a business often means putting your ideas, your passion, and ultimately, yourself, out into the world for public consumption and to be critique. The fear of being judged, ridiculed, or misunderstood by peers, family, or the market can be incredibly intimidating. This fear can cause you to play it safe, avoid innovative ideas, or even abandon their ventures prematurely if they encounter initial negative feedback.

Fear of the Unknown

Entrepreneurship is inherently a journey into uncharted territory. There's no guaranteed roadmap, no steady paycheck, and often, no clear path forward. The uncertainty of financial stability, market acceptance, and future challenges can trigger deep-seated anxieties. This fear often results in a reluctance to take necessary risks, a preference for sticking to familiar but less impactful strategies, or an inability to adapt to changing circumstances.

Fear of Financial Ruin

For many, starting a business involves significant financial risk, often personal savings, loans, or even leveraging assets. The prospect of losing everything and facing financial hardship can be a powerful deterrent. This fear can lead to overly conservative decisions, an unwillingness to invest in growth opportunities, or an inability to weather lean periods, ultimately stifling potential.

How Fear Paralyzes Progress

These fears don't just exist as abstract concepts; they translate into tangible behaviors that actively hinder entrepreneurial progress.

• **Analysis Paralysis**: Over-researching, over-planning, and perpetually seeking more information without ever taking decisive action. The fear of making the wrong choice becomes so intense that no choice is made.

• **Procrastination:** Delaying important tasks, setting arbitrary deadlines that are then missed, or focusing on trivial matters instead of high-impact activities. This often stems from a fear of starting something difficult or unknown.

• **Self-Sabotage:** Unconsciously undermining your own efforts through poor decisions, missed opportunities, or destructive habits as you approach success. This can be a manifestation of the fear of success.

• **Maintaining the Status Quo:** Sticking to comfort zones, even when you are no longer serving the business. This aversion to change or growth is often rooted in the fear of the unknown or fear of failure.

• **Isolation:** A reluctance to network, to seek mentorship, or collaborate, driven by the fear of judgment or revealing perceived weaknesses. This can deny entrepreneurs crucial support and insights.

The cumulative effect of these behaviors is a stalled venture, an unfulfilled dream, and a persistent sense of frustration and regret. But it doesn't have to be this way. In the next section I will give you a few ideas to help you get started to overcome FERA!!

The Path to Overcoming Fear and Moving Forward

Conquering fear isn't about eradicating it entirely; it's about acknowledging its presence, understanding its roots, and developing strategies to move forward despite its whispers. Fear is a natural human emotion; the goal is to prevent it from becoming a dominant force.

1. Acknowledge and Identify Your Fears

The first step is to bring your fears into the light. What exactly are you afraid of? Is it public failure? Financial loss? The weight of responsibility? Write them down. Naming your fears gives you power over them; they become tangible obstacles you can address, rather than amorphous threats.

2. Redefine Failure

Shift your perspective. In entrepreneurship, failure is rarely a definitive end; it's almost always a beginning – a beginning of new learning, new insights, and new strategies. View every setback as a valuable lesson, a data point that informs you of your next move. Adopt the mindset of an experimental scientist: every "failed" experiment simply tells you what doesn't work, bringing you closer to what does.

3. Embrace Imperfection and Action Over Perfection

The pursuit of perfection is often a manifestation of fear of judgment or failure. It leads to endless tweaking and hesitation. Understand that "done is better than perfect." Launch your minimum viable product (MVP), get feedback, and iterate. Taking imperfect action builds momentum and provides real-world data that far outweighs theoretical planning.

4. Break Down Goals into Small, Manageable Steps

An overwhelming goal can trigger immense fear. Break your grand vision into bite-sized, achievable tasks. Focus on completing just the next small step. Each completed step builds confidence and chips away at the overall intimidation factor. This also makes the fear seem less daunting because you're only tackling a tiny portion of the unknown at a time.

5. Build a Strong Support System

You don't have to do this alone. Surround yourself with mentors, fellow entrepreneurs, and a supportive network who understand the challenges. Share your fears and struggles; you'll find that many others feel the same way. A strong network can provide encouragement, advice, and accountability, helping to avoid feelings of isolation and inadequacy.

6. Cultivate a Growth Mindset

Believe that your abilities and intelligence can be developed through dedication and hard work. A growth mindset views challenges as opportunities for growth, rather than insurmountable barriers. It allows you to embrace learning from mistakes and setbacks, seeing them as part of the journey to mastery.

7. Practice Self-Compassion

Be as kind and understanding to yourself as you would be to a friend facing similar challenges. Entrepreneurship is tough, and you will make mistakes. Self-criticism fueled by fear can be debilitating. Acknowledge your efforts, forgive your missteps, and recognize your worth beyond your business's status.

8. Focus on Your "Why"

Reconnect with the core motivation behind your entrepreneurial venture. What problems are you solving? What impact do you want to make? When fear takes hold, centering on your purpose can provide the profound conviction needed to push through discomfort and doubt. Your "why" is your fuel, your North Star.

9. Celebrate Small Victories

Acknowledge and celebrate every small achievement, no matter how minor. Finishing a difficult task, gaining a new client, overcoming a technical hurdle – these small wins build momentum and reinforce positive neural pathways, proving to your brain that action leads to positive outcomes. This counteracts the negative feedback loop that fear often creates.

10. Develop Resilience

Understand that setbacks are inevitable. Resilience is the capacity to bounce back from adversity. Cultivate it by viewing challenges as temporary and learning opportunities, maintaining perspective, and focusing on what you can control. The more you recover from setbacks, the less potent the fear of failure becomes.

11. The Power of Visualization

Regularly visualizing yourself successfully navigating challenges and achieving your goals. See yourself making the tough decisions, overcoming the obstacles, and enjoying the fruits of your labor. This mental rehearsal can reprogram your mind, help in building confidence and reducing the anxiety associated with the unknown.

Conclusion

Fear is an inherent part of the entrepreneurial landscape. It's a primal alarm system, designed to keep us safe. However, in the context of building a business, it often becomes an overprotective parent, stifling growth, and innovation. The most successful entrepreneurs are not fearless; they are individuals who have learned to acknowledge their fears, understand their origins, and develop a robust arsenal of strategies to move forward despite them.

Your journey is a unique story, and fear might be a recurring character, but it doesn't have to be the protagonist. By embracing action over inertia, learning from every experience, and building a supportive ecosystem around you, you can transform fear from a paralyzing force into a powerful motivator. Take that first step, then the next, then the next one, then the next one and watch as the path ahead starts to become clear, not because the fear is gone, but because your resolve to succeed has become infinitely stronger.

~Tuesday Goodson~

Hi everyone, my name is Tuesday Goodson. I am a Managing Director at APLGO. With over three decades of experience in direct sales. My extensive career has been marked by both significant successes and valuable learning experiences, all of which fuels my passion for empowering others to achieve their full potential.

I am a firm believer in the power of perseverance, advocating strongly against letting fear impede on one's business journey—a lesson I openly share from my own path. My dedication to guiding others, I cherish my role as a Nona, wife, and mother, finding joy in many hobbies and watching all kinds of sports.

~ Chapter 13~

Do You Have What It Takes to Be an entrepreneur?

Rosemary Ghiz

Do you have what it takes to be an entrepreneur? Entrepreneurial Secrets? what are they and what exactly does it take to be an entrepreneur? Unknowingly, many entrepreneurs do not even realize they are. They just evolve and grow up with that mindset. It's the way we grow up, the people we surround ourselves with. Entrepreneurs are readers and constant learners, visionaries, and people with big ideas. Entrepreneurs plan and operate their own business or businesses. They are willing to take on risks to achieve their dreams. They visualize their ideas and work through a plan to achieve it. They also surround themselves with like-minded people, who are where they want to be and can help them with their growth.

Who do you know who is doing what you want to be doing and have been successful at it? There are a few characteristics of true entrepreneurs which include passion, creativity, adaptability, leadership with a strong risk tolerance along with a growth mindset and being resilient. They do not allow fear to intervene as they strongly believe in what they want. They also to not express out loud to those they know to be negative and try to talk them out of the idea.

Dismissing it as not feasible, too risky, or too expensive to venture into. These people think they are trying to protect you, but they cannot do it themselves and are fearful of the results or commitment required to achieve the goal. Entrepreneurs when born are faced with this and surrounded by entrepreneurship with business owner mind set in them. Take my own situation as an example. From birth, my father was an entrepreneur business own but there was no word for it at the time. It was just the way it was. My father owned a business along with investment rental properties. Another clue to entrepreneurship, as he had multiple sources of income. This lifestyle was all I knew, growing up in a restaurant seeing my dad working every day to provide a legacy for his family, along with being a real estate investor. What was different to me was that my father didn't go to a job everyday like friends' fathers did so that was different. Many of my relatives were also business owners, so to me that was the normal…

I never realized it growing up, but he was pruning us to be entrepreneurs just like him. It was just a natural way of things. Starting a business and coming up with new ideas and investing our money. Looking for opportunities to grow and never relying on others for our success in life. Entrepreneurs are not taught top see or find opportunities but are big picture thinkers and constantly coming up with ideas as they see the world around them.

They may see a problem and then figure out a way to solve it. My father loved looking at real estate and once when I saw a house for sale, that I loved, he responded with, then figure out how to buy it. No offer to help with the financing, just figure it out on my own. These messages taught me to be resourceful, and risk tolerance became second nature to me. Growing up surrounded by this mindset and business owners shaped my thinking about working and building businesses, which then became the direction I lived my life by.

My first business as it turned out was to my father's delight was to become a real estate agent. Just to be clear, it was not planned, it just evolved from who I was and what my passion was. Entrepreneurism is not for everyone, it's a journey. It takes discipline and perseverance behind being your own boss. You are responsible for your own success or failure and have only yourself to be accountable.

I did though have family and relatives that encouraged me, and that is very important to your success. I learnt early on, not to discuss any ideas of a business to just anyone. As some will will try to talk you down, thinking they are helping you. When I look back on my growing up, I didn't realize it at the time, that mindset, beliefs, and values are all different. I had friends who parents worked hard, and saving was very important. For instance, saving money for a comfortable retirement or saving for that special vacation. This contradicted everything I had learned and the way I was living my life.

Growing up I saw families with strong goals of paying off their mortgages. They did this to be mortgage free, while at the same time they were incurring debts, like, car loans, multiple credit cards, student, and education loans and struggling with paying off bills.

While in my later career as a mortgage broker, I learned the importance of utilizing your homes equity to clear off and consolidate these outside debts. This saves money and gets rid of high interest debts, using the homes equity with a mortgage. Again, it goes back to mind set and what you grew up believing. I remember people telling me with pride that they did not have a mortgage on their home and were not prepared to add a mortgage payment, along with their other debts, even though they were at high interest rates. These same people were saving their money to do home renovations and improvements and just did not have the ability to save money to reinvest.

Money should not be a mission but a by-product to achieve better things in life. Being an entrepreneur is a lifelong identity, whether its inherited of discovered, is a drive to build, lead and create deep internal paths that don't go away. Here are a few top secrets to entrepreneurial longevity, and what keep them going. They evolve and stay ahead, by reinventing themselves. They are constant learners and change with the times. They read the trends, listen, and adapt to what's going on around them and the world at large.

They consistently make changes and pivot with the times. Its not about selling but building systems. They Invest in their growth as much as just doing or running a business. Always looking for new ideas and solving problems. Here are some top secrets of entrepreneurial success and do you have them. Successful entrepreneurs know exactly where they want to go and are prepared to set actionable goals to get there.

They are driven by passion and persistence and believe in their mission. Setbacks are inevitable but what matters is the ability to bounce back even stronger and learn from the setback. Entrepreneurs can pivot with change in the market and adjust to it. Success comes from learning and coming up with new ideas. I was a constant learner staying ahead of the many changes we have. Particularly for me, was the constant change with technology.

True entrepreneurs are disciplined and focused on their ideas and focused on achieving them. They do not work alone but build teams that are like mined and complimentary to building a successful business. Entrepreneurs understand customer needs and the problems they face and are continually improving their plans. Entrepreneurs, are as I mentioned earlier, are continual learnings and stay informed about trends, and particularly technology. Technology that as we know is constantly evolving. So, the question I have for you. Are you an entrepreneur and do you have what it takes to be an entrepreneur?

~Rosemary Ghiz~

Rosemary Ghiz is a seasoned Mortgage Professional, Trainer, Speaker, and 3x Best-Selling Author with over 25- years of experience helping Canadians achieve their homeownership dreams. Her deep industry knowledge, combined with her passion for empowering clients, has made her a trusted expert in the mortgage and finance space. From first-time homebuyers to seasoned homeowners, Rosemary specializes in guiding individuals through the complexities of financing, ensuring they make informed and confident financial decisions.

As a dynamic leader and educator, Rosemary is committed to breaking down the barriers of traditional thinking around money and mortgages. She believes that homeownership isn't just about securing a loan—it's about financial empowerment and long-term security. Her expertise, honed over decades of working with clients and training professionals, allows her to simplify the mortgage process while providing strategic insights that help individuals build wealth and stability. Whether through her books, speaking engagements, or one-on-one consultations, Rosemary is dedicated to providing others with the knowledge and confidence to take control of their financial future.

www.rosemary.ghiz@gmail.com

~ ABOUT THE AUTHOR~

Marianne Padjan Is an International Award-winning Author and Coach. Marianne has received many prestigious awards and excels in all she does. Marianne is also a real estate agent and a Managing Director at APLGO. Marianne is also the CEO at MPowered Voice Publishing. Marianne is a leader of many hats and has made her mark in all places she goes. Marianne holds monthly summits and speaking events regularly.

To get in touch with Rev. Dr. Marianne Padjan please contact her below:

Spiritualtouch11@gmail.com

ENTREPRENEUR SECRETS